NOTORIOUS
ARKANSAS SWINDLER
DR. JOHN KIZER

NOTORIOUS
ARKANSAS SWINDLER
DR. JOHN KIZER

MEDICINE AND MURDER

RODNEY HARRIS

THE
History
PRESS

Published by The History Press
Charleston, SC
www.historypress.com

All images courtesy of Randolph County Heritage Museum.

First published 2024

Manufactured in the United States

ISBN 9781467154963

Library of Congress Control Number: 2023945825

Notice: The information in this book is true and complete to the best of our knowledge. It is offered without guarantee on the part of the authors or The History Press. The author and The History Press disclaim all liability in connection with the use of this book.

This book is dedicated to my sons, Trae and Will Harris.
They keep life interesting.

CONTENTS

ACKNOWLEDGEMENTS

I am grateful for the staff of dedicated volunteers at the Randolph County Heritage Museum in Pocahontas, Arkansas, as well as the staff at the Dean B. Ellis Library at Arkansas State University and at the Arkansas State Archives in Little Rock for all of their assistance in researching this book.

I want to thank my wife, Kristi, and my sons, Trae and Will, for their patience as I have spent time working on this project, and my colleagues at Williams Baptist University for their help and understanding during this process.

I also want to thank my parents, Carl and JoAnn Harris. Without their constant support and encouragement, I would not be where I am today. Lastly, I want to acknowledge Evelyn Fender, my eighth-grade history teacher, who introduced this story to me many years ago. Mrs. Fender helped inspire me to be a history teacher.

INTRODUCTION

By nature, people are drawn to macabre and gruesome stories. The popularity of "true crime" television and podcasts testifies to the love of this genre today. While such crimes are often associated with urban areas, small rural communities, such as Pocahontas and Randolph County, Arkansas, are far from immune. The "Local Crime" exhibit at the Randolph County Heritage Museum in Pocahontas remains a favorite of visitors. The museum attracts thousands of visitors each year from the region, the state, the nation and the world. Many visitors marvel at how a small community can have experienced many notorious crimes and misdeeds. Visitors are drawn to the stories of robberies, bootlegging, murders and lynchings that have taken place in this rural corner of Northeast Arkansas.

The brutal lynching of George Cheverie stands out among the crimes committed in Pocahontas's history. Cheverie and his family—his wife and four children—lived on a houseboat on the Black River. This was not uncommon at the time. Houseboats could be found on the Black and White Rivers and other rivers. The people who lived on these boats were generally poor and scraped out a meager living by fishing, hunting and harvesting mussel shells, which they then sold to small factories for the production of buttons. These people were often labeled "river rats" and seen as less-than-equal citizens. The typical houseboat was roughly ten feet wide and about fifty feet long. They were not mass produced, so no two houseboats were alike, though they were similar. These "homes" did not provide the finer comforts of life and had no sanitary facilities. The

Left: The Cheverie family on their houseboat on the Black River at Pocahontas.

Opposite: Houseboats on the Black River at Pocahontas.

occupants disposed of their waste in the river, the same river out of which they retrieved drinking water and wash water. Local communities saw these river rats as a nuisance, though they often purchased fish and other game from the occupants.[1]

Like many river rats, George Cheverie and his family survived by various means. He sold the fish he caught to the people of Pocahontas. Cheverie's houseboat was tied along the Pocahontas waterfront, not far from the sawmills that provided sustenance for many in the community. To the east of Pocahontas, in the delta where the Current, Black and Fouche Rivers flowed, were vast areas of old-growth timber. As this timber was cleared, great fortunes were made. The trees were cut and dragged by mules to tramways that transported the logs to nearby rivers to float downriver to Pocahontas and other sawmills. In 1909, Joe and Ray Sallee opened a handle mill near this location to take advantage of the ready supply of timber from east of Pocahontas. Often, these logs were lashed together into "rafts." This helped the logs float downriver, where they were retrieved. Naturally, some logs were lost, some became waterlogged and sank and others became trapped in snags or turns in the river. Cheverie and others made extra income by collecting these lost logs and selling them.[2]

Cheverie and Pocahontas town marshal John Norris exchanged words over a log raft like those just mentioned. A raft of logs had struck the Cheverie

houseboat, causing some damage. Cheverie sought to keep the logs to raise funds to repair his houseboat. The owner of these logs disagreed. The town marshal attempted to defuse the situation, and the two men exchanged words. Late on March 20, 1902, Norris tried to approach the Cheverie houseboat, and Cheverie shot and killed the marshal. As news spread, the people of Pocahontas and the surrounding areas became enraged. Cheverie was arrested and taken to the two-story Randolph County Jail one block off Pocahontas Court Square.[3]

Norris had been a popular member of the community, and he left behind a wife and four children. He had also been a member of the local chapter of the Knights of Pythias, a fraternal organization. The Knights of Pythias were founded in Washington, D.C., in 1864 as a secret society, and Pocahontas boasted a significant chapter. The knights met at their local lodge hall on the second floor of a building across the street from the Randolph County Courthouse, and tempers flared. Cheverie had been indicted on a murder charge, but due to the community's anger, the examination trial was postponed to let tempers cool. This angered many in the community. When the lodge meeting ended, many men moved next door to the Turner Saloon and continued to discuss the situation. As the night wore on and these men drank more and more, they also became emboldened. A plan was hatched to remove Cheverie from jail and bring him to swift "justice." Late in the night, between four hundred and five hundred men gathered on the court square before walking one block, where they broke Cheverie out of jail. This task was easier said than done and required men to use makeshift ramrods to bust down the jail door. The law enforcement officers in the jail fought back valiantly, but to no avail. One member of the crowd later died from injuries he sustained when the ramrod returned, hitting him in the stomach and causing internal injuries. The lynch mob took Cheverie from jail and lynched him. Cheverie was hanged from a steel bridge over the Marr Creek near the square. The condemned man's body was left hanging until midmorning as an example of vigilante justice—in other words, to put fear into citizens' minds. The George Cheverie lynching remains one of only two such crimes in the county. The other, the lynching of George Cole, took place in 1872. Both men were white.[4]

SALLEE BROTHERS HANDLE MILL IN 1914

Sallee Handle Mill, Pocahontas, Arkansas.

In 1931, another infamous act took place in Pocahontas. Manley Jackson, the night marshal for Pocahontas, was found murdered. His body was discovered roughly five miles outside of town. Jackson had been shot execution-style four times in the back. The case took a strange turn when two local men, Lige Dame and Earl Decker, were accused of murdering Jackson. The story became stranger when the men implicated John Slayton, the former chief of police in Pocahontas. Both men were indicted for Jackson's murder. On the stand, Dame and Decker recounted a convoluted tale. According to Dame, his wife and Jackson had been having an affair, which led Dame and his associate to kill the lawman. Their story did not end there. Both men further claimed that Slayton also wanted Jackson dead. According to the two confessed murderers, the police chief paid them $500 to murder Jackson. Both Dame and Decker were convicted of the murder of Jackson. John Slayton was charged and tried. The trial of the former police chief drew broad interest, with seats in the courtroom selling for as high as $2 to hear the testimony of Dame. On the stand, Dame indicated that Slayton had offered the pair as much as $1,000 to kill Jackson. No motive was given for wanting Jackson killed. The jury struggled to reach a verdict in Slayton's trial but eventually convicted him as an accessory. Slayton was found guilty and sentenced to life. Despite this sentence, he was allowed to post a bond of $25,000 pending an appeal for his conviction to the Arkansas Supreme Court. In 1932, that court overturned Slayton's conviction in *Slayton v. State*. Two attempts were made to retry Slayton, both resulting in hung juries. Both Dame and Decker served time in the Arkansas Penitentiary for the murder of Manley Jackson.[5]

Following his conviction, Dame recanted his confession. Both men maintained their innocence. In 1971, Alvin Karpis published a memoir, *The Alvin Karpis Story*. A member of the Ma Barker Gang, Karpis had been serving a life sentence for the kidnapping of William Hamm Jr. in Minneapolis when he was released after thirty-three years in 1968. In 1971, Karpis recounted his life of crime and briefly mentioned Pocahontas, Arkansas. He told how the gang stopped in the town one night in 1931. Manley Jackson found their car suspicious avnd jotted down its license plate number. Shortly after this, the gang forced Jackson to get into their car.

They took the notepad with their plate number from him and drove him five miles outside of town, where they executed him in a gravel pit. Pocahontas had a brush with the Ma Barker Gang and did not know about it for forty years. So many mysteries remain concerning this case. Why did Dame and Decker claim they killed Jackson? Why did they implicate the chief of police? This story remains one of Pocahontas's stranger "true crime" stories.[6]

Crimes involving women draw greater interest and scrutiny. This is true of the Cora Hebner case in Randolph County. Hebner has been described as an "ethereal beauty" from Clinton, Illinois. After high school, she enrolled at the University of Illinois, though she did not remain a student long. Cora quickly met a man, one of the many who would establish a common theme in her life. The man she met, Samuel Sullivan, wooed her at a school dance with tales of his world travels. He convinced the beautiful young woman to marry him that night. Following their elopement, they boarded a train to St. Louis, where they began their honeymoon. Sullivan, a shyster with little to no money, essentially trapped Cora. Shortly after they arrived in St. Louis, he pressured her to prostitute herself to provide for the couple financially. She

Ma Barker of the Ma Barker Gang. The gang killed Manley Jackson in Pocahontas.

refused, and Sullivan became enraged. He abandoned her in St. Louis, but she refused to return home. After all, Cora had written many letters to her parents and friends, making her new life sound amazing. She could not bear to face them now that it had fallen apart so quickly, though she was still married to Sullivan.[7]

The experience with Sullivan started Cora on a life of deceit. In 1902, she married Guy Wayne Butts, a prominent real estate promoter in St. Louis. She was well aware that the marriage was not legal. She was still married to Sullivan; Butts had no clue he existed. This relationship lasted five years before ending in divorce. The settlement left Cora with $10,000 in cash and a small home in her name. With her newfound financial security, she began entertaining a series of wealthy men who were more than willing to pay for whatever Cora wanted, and she wanted plenty. Next, Cora met Eduardo Trueba, a wealthy landowner from Mexico. Trueba fell madly in love with Cora. She soon traveled to Mexico City with her new beau. Not long after this, they married, and Cora began to think she needed to find Sullivan and end her marriage. This desire led her to place advertisements inquiring about her first husband, her only legal husband. Soon enough, he responded to her ad but sought to blackmail her with the knowledge that he was her lawful spouse. Sullivan wanted her to leave her husband. He said he would disclose her previous marriage if she didn't. He also wanted her money and property. Rather than come clean to Trueba, she told him she wanted a divorce. The catch was that the husband's name was Will Hebner; Samuel had been his alias. Will spent Cora's money, took over her home and property and even paraded young women through the house.[8]

When the couple's money ran low, the Hebners sold Cora's property in St. Louis and purchased a farm in rural Randolph County near Pocahontas. The couple began a scheme by advertising as a lonely widow or widower looking for a new mate. They apparently received numerous responses and did homework to determine which respondents were wealthy enough to invest their time in fleecing. While Will seemed to do most of the fleecing, it is known that Cora married at least two men during this period, Otto Behn of Montana and Joseph Heiker of Oklahoma. During this period, she and Will traveled extensively and seldom spent time together. Many of these trips centered on relieving men and women of their assets. In 1937, Will Hebner left Pocahontas on a trip; he never returned. At first, no one questioned his absence. After all, he was often away.[9]

In time, though, rumors began to spread. Some said Will had left Cora, while more persistent rumors alleged that Cora had killed her husband and buried him in an old cellar on their farm. These rumors persisted until the sheriff was forced to investigate, forcing Cora to produce a letter allegedly written by Will. The letter had been mailed from Tulsa, Oklahoma, and in it he assured Cora that he would return to her side soon. Shortly after this letter, Cora sold her farm and fled Pocahontas. The new owners quickly discovered Will, buried in the cellar, just as people had suspected. The discovery of Will led to a search for Cora. Despite her efforts to conceal her getaway, the sheriff traced her to St. Louis and a man. She had spent a night with him before disappearing once again. Investigators discovered that Cora had rented a storage facility in St. Louis, and the bills were sent to an address in Miami, Florida. In Florida, she was up to her old games, placing ads in a magazine looking for unsuspecting lonely men. Cora was returned to Pocahontas, where she was placed in the Randolph County Jail. While in jail, she committed suicide using a small vial of poison.[10]

No "true crime" case in Randolph County and Pocahontas draws as much attention as that of John R. Kizer. The Kizer story attracted plenty of attention locally and across the nation as his trial drew near. Newspapers across the country carried accounts of the murdering veterinarian. These stories ran in the *Poplar Bluff Republican*, the *Chattanooga News*, the *St. Louis Post-Dispatch* and the *Clarion-Ledger* of Jackson, Mississippi. The most common account of Kizer's string of murders claims that he killed ten people before taking his own life with poison, much as Cora Hebner did in jail. This version was made famous in 1957 by Charles Morehead, who wrote for *True Detective* magazine. This publication was a precursor of today's true crime genre.[11]

True Detective was published from 1924 until 1995. The publication reached its peak in the 1940s, '50s and '60s. The magazine sold millions of copies and initiated a "true crime" fixation that remains today. Throughout the history of the publication, the boundaries between fiction and fact were often blurred. When Bernarr Macfadden began publishing the magazine, the focus was on fiction, with the occasional nonfiction article thrown into the mix. By the mid-1930s, the focus allegedly had moved to nonfiction, though there seems to be some doubt if this move was exclusive. In 1957, Charles Morehead wrote "They Died Like Dogs," a version of the John R. Kizer story. This version of the tale quickly became the accepted take on the events surrounding Kizer.[12]

Little is known of Morehead and his journalistic legacy. He admits that he changed at least one name in the story. A close examination of the Morehead version of Kizer and his crimes leads to more questions than answers. Unfortunately, this version has become the dominant one. The

Randolph County Heritage Museum Archives contain an unpublished manuscript covering the last days of Kizer's life. Written by an unknown author, "John R. Kizer: A Judgement Call" is heavily influenced by the Morehead version of events. A more recent article, "For the Love of Money," appeared in *AY Magazine*, a Little Rock, Arkansas–based publication that followed the accepted story, further establishing the tale, warts and all, in the local history. The local museum on Court Square in Pocahontas and its parent organization, Five Rivers Historic Preservation Inc., have done their part in hosting ghost tours and speakers who addressed elements of the Kizer story. This book began as an effort to tell the John Kizer story to a broader audience. It quickly became apparent that the John R. Kizer story had taken on folklore status as it was passed down over time and could not be substantiated in totality. It is common for historical tour scripts and ghost stories to evolve and change. What seems odd is the fact that the Kizer story underwent substantial changes just two decades after some of the events took place. Many in Randolph County and Pocahontas simply sought to forget the story. Lawrence Dalton, the undisputed historian of Randolph County, failed to make mention of Kizer or his murders in his history published in the 1940s. This discovery that the accepted story contains significant discrepancies leaves major questions that must be answered. Who did Kizer murder? How many people did he kill? How did this story take on a life of its own?[13]

COMPLICATED POCAHONTAS

R andolph County and Pocahontas, the county seat, are located in a complicated place, geographically. The county and the city straddle two of Arkansas's six geographic regions. The portion of the county and city northwest of the Black and Current Rivers is firmly in the Arkansas Ozarks, while the region southeast of the rivers is part of the Arkansas Delta ("the Delta"). This division is stark at times. The earliest human visitors to what is today Randolph County were participants in Native American hunting expeditions, most likely Osage hunters from southern Missouri. While earlier histories claim Hernando de Soto traversed the county in 1541, no historical evidence shows that his expedition ever reached the region. Historian Lawrence Dalton refers to early settlers at Pitman finding Spanish coins. It is worth noting, however, that Spanish coins were widely used, and this discovery means simply that either Native Americans who had come in contact with Europeans left these coins or that an earlier group of Europeans crossed the Current River at this location.[14]

The region that became modern-day Randolph County served as an essential gateway for westward expansion following the Louisiana Purchase. Once again, the region's geographic location played a prominent role. Many migrants viewed Arkansas as a troublesome wasteland that had to be crossed on the way to Texas and elsewhere, while others settled in Arkansas. Migration from much of Tennessee and Mississippi was complicated by the strip of swampy land on the state's eastern border along the Mississippi River. Present-day Randolph County provided a better route for migration.

In 1803, William Hix established a ferry crossing on the Current River in the extreme northeast corner of the county. This crossing and the Southwest Trail made Randolph County an ideal gateway for migrants from Kentucky, Missouri, Illinois and Tennessee. By entering at Hix Ferry, settlers avoided the swamps of eastern Arkansas. Without a doubt, St. Louis was the gateway to the American West, but Hix Ferry should be seen as an essential entry point for migrants.[15]

It is not known who rightfully claimed the title of the first white settler in Randolph County. However, it is known that around 1800, Dr. William Jarrett purchased a land claim from Richard Fletcher in the Columbia area of the county. John Gould Fletcher, the Pulitzer Prize–winning poet from Arkansas, descended from this family. Around the same time, John Janes settled in the county's western portion along the creek that bears his name. A veteran of the American Revolution, Janes purportedly saw action at Yorktown before migrating west. Janes first settled in St. Louis before moving to Arkansas.[16]

When the first settlers entered Randolph County, they found a vast wilderness traversed by five rivers. These rivers provided water for settlers, livestock and wild game and became early highways for the new migrants. The early settlements within what is now Randolph County were all located along these streams and relied on them for commerce and sustenance.

In 1811, Dr. Peyton R. Pitman purchased the Hix Ferry and established a profitable business and farm. The Southwest Trail entered Randolph County at the ferry. The trail was the primary route for migrants traveling from St. Louis and Ste. Genevieve to Arkansas, Texas and even Mexico. The town of Pitman was established in 1820 and quickly became an economic hub in the region. In 1826, the Mount Pleasant Baptist Church was established in Pitman and remains one of the oldest congregations in the state. Present-day Randolph County attracted some interesting historical figures, such as Louis de Mun. Most accounts assert that de Mun was born on a ship as his family traveled between France and Saint Dominique, making the young man an adventurer from birth. He was educated in France and exiled following the French Revolution. Between 1813 and 1816, de Mun lived in Arkansas, making his home at Davidsonville. He also operated a mill just outside of present-day Pocahontas.[17]

In 1815, Davidsonville was established near the confluence of the Spring, Eleven Point and Black Rivers. At its founding, the town served as a stop on the Southwest Trail, and the settlement grew. Davidsonville was the first town in Arkansas to be designed on a street grid. Many firsts in Arkansas history happened at Davidsonville. The settlement was the home to the first post office in the state, the first federal land office and the first courthouse built in Arkansas. When the Southwest Trail became the Military Road, it bypassed Davidsonville, hurting the town. Shortly after this, the land office was moved to Batesville on the White River, and the courthouse moved multiple times before being located in the new village of Pocahontas following a countywide vote.[18]

In 1815, Ransom S. Bettis migrated with other extended family members from Greenville, Missouri. Bettis established a trading post called Bettis Bluff along the Black River upriver from Davidsonville. When Randolph County was established in 1835, two communities sought the distinction of being the county seat, Fourche De Thomas (Columbia) and Bettis Bluff (Pocahontas). Ransom Bettis, the founder of present-day Pocahontas, with the help of his son-in-law Thomas S. Drew, knew that the survival of their settlement was contingent on becoming the county seat. The two men hatched a plan. In the upcoming countywide vote, ballots could be cast at any polling place in the county. To lure more voters to their cause, Bettis and Drew threw a massive barbecue complete with all the whiskey voters could drink. In the end, Bettis Bluff won the election and secured the county seat.[19]

This extended kinship group provided the basis for Bettis Bluff and Pocahontas. Names associated with this group of migrants still dot the landscape in the region. Names such as Marr, Mansker and others are part of the fabric of Randolph County and Pocahontas. For this kinship group and others, after all, there was safety in numbers, and these families made up the early elites of the county and controlled much of the region's wealth until the Civil War and, in some cases, after.

Rural communities grew as well. In 1828, Reuben Rice constructed a trading post near the Eleven Point River, not far from the present town of Dalton. Rice had migrated to the region in 1812, along with other settlers who were part of an interconnected group of families related by marriage and other kinship bonds and with their enslaved persons. Rice benefited from the enslavement of people and developed his home into a trading center, leading to his amassing significant wealth. The Rice family was known for their production of fabrics, for instance. As his wealth grew, so did his standing in the community. In 1835, Rice was selected as one of the commissioners to oversee the construction of the first courthouse in Pocahontas. Another family group member, William Looney, constructed a log tavern across the Eleven Point River in 1833. Looney, like Rice, owned enslaved persons and amassed a sizable estate by the time he died in 1846.[20]

In 1826, Cinderella Bettis, daughter of Ransom, married Thomas S. Drew. By 1829, Bettis Bluff had become a center for trading. Steamboats like the *Laurel* traveled from the Mississippi River up the White River to the Black River and the port. Some steamboats traveled up the Current River as far as the present-day town of Biggers. Beyond this point, goods were shipped by flatboats and over land. In 1835, the settlement's name was changed from Bettis Bluff to Pocahontas. Little is known about this name change or the origin of the new name. Few, if any, records remain concerning this name change. In 1835, Randolph County was created out of the larger Lawrence County, and the citizens began a debate about the location of the county seat. After the courthouse left Davidsonville in 1829, the court was held at several locations. One legend is that the Columbia folks said Bettis and Drew had "poked it to us" and that the name resulted in Pocahontas.[21]

Thomas Drew's marriage to Cinderella increased his wealth tremendously, as Ransom gave the young couple a plantation as a wedding gift. The home was not a massive manse with white columns, but this was still a tremendous gift. The Drews' wealth grew as they purchased more land and enslaved people. In 1837, Drew donated land for the site of the county courthouse, and he and Bettis platted the town around this square. Over the years, Drew worked as a teacher, a peddler and a lawyer, along with being a planter and land speculator. While some historians have questioned Drew's many professions, it is not outside the norm for a place like Arkansas. Drew, like many of the other leading men of his day, would have worked any job or profession that allowed him to advance his goal. For instance, teaching school for a term or more while one prepared for a legal career was considered perfectly acceptable for an aspiring gentleman.[22]

In March 1831, Congress approved funding to build a military road in Arkansas. This road would follow the Southwest Trail, the same path that Native Americans and settlers had traveled for many years. This trail ran along the foothills of the Ozark Mountains, far enough from the river bottoms to avoid flooding yet far enough from the higher ground that made travel difficult. Over the years, a significant number of migrants traversed this road. Historian Lawrence Dalton cites men such as Sam Houston, Davy Crockett, Henry Schoolcraft and Ulysses S. Grant as having passed through the region and using the Pitman Ferry. While many migrants were going to Texas, some remained in the area and helped populate Randolph County. One such traveler was Dr. George Engelmann, a noted German botanist who immigrated to the United States in 1832. He is best known for his diary entries written as he traveled the country. Engelmann traveled through

Randolph County in 1837, making stops in Pitman and other locales. He spent time with Dr. Pitman and wrote about the prosperous ferry, the substantial Pitman home and the surrounding farmland.[23]

By 1829, the port of Pocahontas was a dynamic economic hub with steamboats traveling from the Mississippi River up the White and Black Rivers and up the Current River as far as present-day Biggers. This river traffic helped fuel the country's growing economy and helped Pocahontas become a leading economic center in the region. Thomas Drew's prominence grew as well. In 1844, he became "the family" nominee for governor of Arkansas. At the time, the Arkansas Democratic Party was controlled by a group of families related by blood and marriage who would hold control until the Civil War. In 1844, this group had trouble finding a candidate suitable to all the factions within the group, and they eventually agreed on Drew. Once elected, Drew discovered that he did not really like the governor's office and that it was a financial hardship due to the low salary. This financial strain was evident in 1846, when Drew sold a sizable property at the juncture of Marr Creek and the Black River to William Looney. Drew began selling assets, and his wealth began a precarious decline from which he would not recover. Drew was nominated for a second term and won but resigned shortly after due to the job's low pay. He was plagued by debt for the remainder of his life and slowly sold his investments, including his enslaved persons, before moving to Texas, where he died.[24]

The town was developing as well. In 1853, William Allaire constructed the St. Charles Hotel on the east side of Court Square. What was once a rustic frontier village was evolving into a town, and this growth continued until the outbreak of the Civil War. Other communities were taking shape as well. In 1857, Dennis Reynolds settled near Drew's former plantation, Cherokee Bay, and opened a mercantile business that would prove successful. In the coming years, this became the town of Reyno. Just before the outbreak of the Civil War, Lewis Dalton settled on the Eleven Point River near his namesake town.[25]

Randolph County suffered like many border communities during the Civil War. Writing in the 1940s, historian Lawrence Dalton referred to the war as the "regrettable War Between the States," though he did not embrace the Lost Cause mentality of the era and expressed his happiness that the North won the war.[26]

Once again, geography was to play a central role in the history of Pocahontas and Randolph County. The county's location, where the Ozarks meet the Delta, meant that large sections of land had few enslaved people. The average enslaver would have held only one or two enslaved people, though there were exceptions, such as Thomas Drew and others. Randolph County also bordered southern Missouri. While Missouri would not leave the Union, the state was home to many Southern sympathizers. Arkansas seceded from the Union mainly in response to President Abraham Lincoln's call for troops after the attack on Fort Sumter. Following secession, Confederate leaders in Arkansas worried about an invasion from Missouri and sought to secure the state's northern border. General William J. Hardee was sent to Pocahontas to assume command of a large group of troops. These troops primarily camped along Mill Creek, at Camp Shaver southwest of Pocahontas. Eight companies of soldiers were organized in Randolph County for the Confederacy, and an unknown number of men joined the Union effort. Northern Arkansas was known for its Unionists, and Randolph County was no different. These companies were organized at Pocahontas as well as at Pitman Ferry. On July 20, 1862, a battle was fought near Pitman Ferry. On August 22, 1863, Union forces attacked Confederate forces at Pocahontas, and in September 1863, Confederate troops attacked Union forces near Cherokee Bay. Following the attack on Pocahontas, Union troops occupied the town for several months. During the war, the county experienced a significant amount of "bushwhacking," or guerrilla warfare, which led to suffering of the general population. For example, a contingent of Union troops captured a sizable number of men on a Sunday after they broke up a church service at Siloam Church. For much of the war, Randolph County was a contested space. The town of Pitman Ferry was burned during the war, as was part of Pocahontas.[27]

Following the Civil War, economic recovery in Randolph County and Pocahontas proved slow. The region had been on the borderlands of war and had suffered at the hands of both sides. Pocahontas and other communities were slowly rebuilt, but it took years for the economic activity to reach the levels experienced before the war. In 1868, Father James P. O'Kean, a Confederate veteran and Irish immigrant, traveled through the area. O'Kean met a group of men from Pocahontas, and they invited him to deliver a series of lectures explaining the doctrine of the Catholic Church. These lectures were by all accounts a success, as land was quickly donated to construct a church and money was given for the same purpose. In 1868, St. Paul the Apostle Catholic Church was founded in Pocahontas. Over the next three decades, led by Father Eugene Weibel, growing numbers of Catholic immigrants arrived in Randolph County. The county was eventually home to two parishes, one in Pocahontas and one at Engelberg.[28]

Rural communities continued to grow. Captain John Maynard established a store in the present-day town that bears his name. Initially, the settlement was called "New Prospect." Maynard eventually opened a cotton gin to serve the area, and the town grew over time to accommodate a flour mill, a sawmill, a gristmill, a bank and a newspaper. With the opening of the Abbot Institute, sometimes called Maynard Academy or Ouachita Academy, Maynard became a center of learning within the county.[29]

By the 1870s, the original courthouse at Pocahontas was in bad shape. The county needed to do more to maintain the wooden structure, and it was in danger of falling down. County leaders decided to construct a new courthouse on the square. County leaders had been talking about a new courthouse as early as 1868, and the county began accepting bids in May 1869. After a couple of years of delay, the contract was awarded in April 1872, when John A. McKay of Helena was given the contract. He would be paid $39,865, and the building would be completed by April 1, 1873. Construction, as is often the case, did not go as planned, and McKay was fired. Eventually, the building was completed in 1875. This is the iconic "Old Court House" that stands today.[30]

Randolph County Courthouse, today known as the "old" court house.

Biggers House Hotel.

In 1880, the *Pocahontas Star Herald* began, and it has served the town and county ever since. In fact, it is the oldest continuously operated business in the county. As the community and the economy grew, Pocahontas acquired new amenities. In 1880, B.F. Bigger and his wife, Ida, bought the Heavener Hotel and renamed it the Biggers House. The Biggers House became known for its hospitality and food. The hotel had a large two-story veranda overlooking the waterfront and railroad. Patrons enjoyed relaxing on the porch, or they could descend the steps that led to the train depot and the waterfront. At about the same time, Pocahontas organized the first public school system in the town, which met in the Masonic Lodge until a proper campus could be constructed.[31]

Pocahontas was one of many parts of the county expanding in the 1880s. Dennis Reynolds, who opened a mercantile business some years earlier, prospered. The town of Reyno developed. In 1883, Reynolds purchased a grand piano in New Orleans and shipped it up the Mississippi River to the White River and then to the Black. A barge up the Current River delivered the piano to the Reynolds home. Randolph County and its residents were getting rid of the backwater image and experiencing some of the finer things in life.[32]

The region's citizens had more free time on their hands as well. In 1883, the Southern Hotel opened at Ravenden Springs. This area was known as "Dream Town," partly because of the story of Reverend William Bailey's dream that spring water had health benefits. The area soon developed into a resort town that drew visitors from a wide area. The new town of Ravenden Springs grew rapidly thanks to the tourist industry. In 1903, the Lone Star Bank opened in Ravenden as the town continued to prosper.[33]

One side benefit of economic growth and the loss of the frontier image in Pocahontas was the emergence of churches. In 1885, the Pocahontas Church of Christ was founded and would later become the Pyburn Street Church of Christ. A Methodist congregation was also founded and grew, and the Catholic Church constructed a larger building. In 1899, a group of Baptists organized a church that would eventually become First Baptist Pocahontas. These churches mark a defining moment as Pocahontas shed its rough frontier image and embraced "civilization."[34]

Wooden frame buildings gave way to one- and two-story brick buildings in Pocahontas as the economy grew and the town changed. In 1909, the south side of the square housed Pringle Drug Store, the De Clerk Saloon, a

The *Pocahontas Star Herald* office in the early days.

hotel and other businesses. That year, the Sallee brothers moved their stave mill operation to Pocahontas. They purchased the land at the intersection of Marr Creek and the Black River and built a mill. This meant that they were well suited to use the river to transport timber cut in the forests of the river bottoms east of town and then ship their mill goods to market. The Sallee family quickly became one of the wealthiest in the region and opened an ice company and other businesses. In 1910, the Randolph County Bank opened at the corner of Bettis Street and Broadway on Court Square. This building housed the bank and the Martin insurance agency on the first floor and lawyers' offices on the second floor. Pocahontas and several law firms represented the growing commercial interests of the town. The nature of the square changed with the construction of George Premerger's hardware store on the west side and other buildings. Beginning in 1911, citizens and businesses in Pocahontas could have electric lights after the light and power plant was built near the town's waterfront, and the first trains arrived in 1912. Much of the town's new money was rooted in timber and agricultural interests. By 1915, Pocahontas could boast about the town's new sewer system.[35]

Pocahontas and Randolph County experienced significant change following the Civil War. The region fully embraced the New South and the Progressive Era. John Kizer grew up among and was impacted by much of this change. As the sustenance economy gave way to a capital-centric economy in which many rural farmers were left behind, resentment and sometimes hatred sprang up among the increasingly separated social and economic classes.

2

GROWING UP KIZER

L ike so many families in the years after the Civil War, the Kizer family lived a life of sustenance farming with very little cash, but they succeeded to a great extent. The family lived in a remote region of Randolph County and, like many rural families, did not regularly travel to Pocahontas, the nearest town of any size. But young John Kizer was in awe of all he saw when the family went to town.

During this time, it was common for some rural families to visit Pocahontas just once or twice a year. This did not mean that these families did not rely on store-bought items; instead, these items typically came from the local country store. The men of these rural households often made the trip to town to take care of business and to socialize, leaving the women and children on the farm. One piece of evidence of this phenomenon is the large number of photographs of men taken in photography studios, such as those in Pocahontas, and the sheer lack of photos of women in the same era.

After an initial period of economic stagnation following the Civil War, Pocahontas experienced significant growth. Like many other county-seat towns, Pocahontas fully embraced the New South mantra. Shortly after John Kizer was born in 1872, Randolph County completed the Italianate Randolph County Court House. As a result, Pocahontas experienced substantial economic growth. This growth was evident by the founding of a newspaper, the *Pocahontas Star Herald*; the number of businesses that opened; and the number of hotels, banks and other business establishments that opened. During the same period, Pocahontas organized a public school system.[36]

The population of both Randolph County and Pocahontas grew during these years. When Kizer was born, the county had a population of 7,466. This number would grow to 19,987 by 1900. In Pocahontas, the jump in population is starker. In 1880, the town had a population of only 325. By 1900, the population was 967. One factor contributing to this growth was European immigration. The influx of immigrants was part of a more extensive movement of Roman Catholics and others fleeing religious persecution in Europe. Following the war, Arkansas needed an infusion of capital and people. Like other states, it established offices designed to promote the state to European immigrants. Private organizations participated in these efforts, as did railroad companies. The railroads had been given massive amounts of federal and state land in exchange for building rail lines. Now they needed buyers to purchase these lands. While German Catholic immigration in Arkansas focused on the Arkansas River Valley in towns such as Conway, Morrilton and Russellville, Pocahontas and Randolph County received their fair share.[37]

The Catholic Church has existed in Arkansas since colonial times but without significant influence or success in attracting new members. In 1867, Arkansas still had a small number of priests and only six parishes. In 1868, a church was begun in Pocahontas, but it experienced little growth. Then, in 1879, Father Eugene Weibel came to Pocahontas. Under his leadership, the local church grew, as did the number of Catholic immigrants, such as the Baltz, Barre', Jansen, DeClerk, Peters, Throesch and Thielemeir families. Weibel went on to establish other Catholic parishes in Northeast Arkansas. There is no indication that Kizer had much interaction with this growing Catholic community as a young man, but as he got older and became more involved around Pocahontas, he had more contact.[38]

It is easy to imagine Kizer visiting Pocahontas on a Saturday, the most popular day for farm families to come to town. The bustling Pocahontas Court Square would have demonstrated to the young man the realities of the local economy. The Randolph County Heritage Museum collection shows a photo of Merchants Day from about 1900. The picture shows a packed Pocahontas Court Square with standing room only. Also of interest in the image is a tightrope walker traversing a wire between the courthouse and the west side of the square. This is the Pocahontas that John Kizer would have encountered on his trips to town as a young man.[39]

It is doubtful that John Kizer had money to spend at Skinner's Drug Store or other establishments around the square. This sense of being poor fed Kizer's resentment and his determination to one day have money. Money

Merchants Day around the turn of the twentieth century. Note the tightrope walker.

was tight for the Kizer family, as it was with many rural families. It is easy to imagine town boys looking down on country boys like Kizer. John Kizer grew up resenting this poverty, and this resentment fed his lifelong desire to obtain money and respectability. Despite being born after the Civil War, Kizer grew up in a family that fully embraced the idea that the Confederacy should have won the war; in other words, they had been wronged and their heritage taken from them. Kizer grew up with a chip on his shoulder concerning his and his family's social and economic position. Like many others of the era, the family never managed to get ahead economically.

Between 1871 and 1881, Francis Marion Kizer and Catherine Lane Kizer had six children, three boys and three girls. John Kizer, the second oldest, was born in 1872 on his family's farm near Dalton in Randolph County. John's father, Francis, was born in 1837, meaning he would have been twenty-four years old when the Civil War began. It is unknown when Francis migrated to Missouri. There is also some conflicting evidence about where he lived before moving. In both the 1880 and 1900 censuses, John claimed his father was born in Alabama. In 1910, though, he told the census taker that his dad was born in Tennessee. Later, in the 1920 and 1930 censuses, he claimed that his father was born in Georgia.

Little if anything is known about Kizer's home life. While we know his family led a rough existence, it was not rare. Their neighbors would have lived much the same way. What is unknown is the family dynamic of the Kizer children, especially John. Minus this information, it is impossible to determine if this contributed to Kizer's future misdeeds. It is easy to assume that there would be little downtime and little time for fun on a hill farm of the era.

Francis Marion Kizer variously told census takers that he was born in Alabama in 1860, 1880 and 1900, but in 1910, he declared that he had been born in Tennessee. These discrepancies are likely accidental, and the facts lead to many unanswered questions. Were the Kizers running from something or someone? At this time, before social security numbers, it was not uncommon, nor was it difficult, to move to a new location and change one's name to avoid an unpleasant or inconvenient past.[40]

On June 5, 1861, twenty-three-year-old Francis Marion Kizer enlisted at Columbia, Missouri, as a private in the Fifteenth Missouri Regiment fighting for the Confederacy. This decision aligns with the family's southern roots, whether they were from Tennessee, Alabama, Georgia or Virginia, and it makes sense that they would have been sympathetic with the South. It is not known if they owned enslaved persons in Missouri before the war. More than likely, Francis Marion Kizer, like many young southern men, aspired to more wealth, and that would have meant owning land and enslaved persons. Many young men who fought for the Confederacy did so not to protect their wealth or property—namely, their enslaved property—but to protect what they saw as a path to future wealth, even if they had not been able to participate. He was part of General Sterling Price's unsuccessful cavalry raid through Arkansas, Missouri and Kansas. General Price sought to capture Missouri for the Confederacy and to broaden the conflict. Francis would have seen much of Randolph County as part of this force. A map of Price's campaign indicated that Kizer more than likely spent time in Pocahontas. Price's campaign failed, and many Confederates from Missouri began to ponder their future. It was one thing to enlist, as around forty thousand Missourians did when there appeared to be at least some prospect of Southern victory. But once the war was over, these Southern sympathizers experienced a chilly reception back home. In many cases, they were seen as suspects at best and traitors at worst.[41]

Following the war, like many former Confederates, Francis Marion Kizer sought to move south, where he might find a more welcoming community. On July 23, 1867, Francis married Catherine Lane in Randolph County.

Catherine was born in Ironton, Missouri, in 1842. Francis's father, Julian Kizer, and his mother, whose name is not known, along with Catherine's parents, moved with the family to northern Randolph County. More than likely, the family, like many pro-Confederate families, no longer felt welcome in southern Missouri following the Confederate defeat and moved to Arkansas. The Kizers moved to an area that Francis had at least some knowledge of from his time in the Confederate army.[42]

John Kizer's maternal grandparents died in 1879, when he was eight years old. His paternal grandfather lived until 1917, when he passed away at eighty. These family members are buried at the Reynolds Cemetery near Elm Store, Arkansas, near the Kizer farm.[43]

John Kizer grew up working on the family farm. Francis Kizer was always listed as either a farm laborer or a farmer in the census. By all accounts, the young man was a good worker who took farm life seriously. In 1900, John, twenty-eight, was still living at home, and the census recorded him as a farmer. John loved animals, with one major exception: he hated dogs. The roots of this hatred are unknown, but the boy would nurse a sick animal for days to restore its health, but he would kill a dog. This became a pattern for John. This Jekyll-and-Hyde behavior regarding most animals and dogs is an early sign of his callous disregard for some living creatures. However, at the time, it meant little to those around him. After all, dogs were known to run cattle and cause problems on a farm, so disliking "man's best friend" would not have been a signal of future issues.[44]

A popular account of John Kizer claims that he made a decision at the age of twenty-five to become a veterinarian. But according to the 1900 census, taken when John was twenty-eight, he was still listed as a farmer. More than likely, he slowly made the transition and farmed at the same time he began working as a veterinarian. This decision was a natural one, since he had nursed many barnyard animals back to health and showed an aptitude for working with animals—except dogs. At the time, no degree or significant training was required to become a veterinarian.

On September 7, 1902, John Kizer married a local divorcée, Birdie Brooks. The 1910 census lists her as Burdie, but her name appears to have been spelled "Birdie." When they married, she was thirty-six years old, six years older than John. William Brooks and Birdie had married in Ripley County, Missouri, in 1880. At the time of their marriage, William owned more than 546 acres in Randolph and Lawrence Counties, Arkansas. He ran a successful farming operation and was involved in Democratic politics in the state. The couple had five children before they divorced following the birth of their last child in 1890. The reason for their divorce is not known. In a 1957 edition of *True Detective*, Charles Morehead claimed that Birdie was a widow with a modest inheritance. But census records, death records and other sources do not support this assertion. William did not remarry after his divorce, and he passed away in 1925.[45]

After marriage, John and Birdie moved to Pocahontas with the three Brooks children. Kizer had never owned a home. He had lived with his parents until his marriage. The young couple joined the new county extension service created by Congress's Smith-Lever Act in 1914. The act established a partnership between land grant universities such as the University of Arkansas and the U.S. Department of Agriculture. The Kizers became the first county agents for Randolph County. As county agent, John instructed farmers on how to raise crops and care for livestock and assisted with issues such as crop rotation and fertilization. Birdie taught women canning and food preparation and skills such as mattress making. In this sense, the Kizers were part of the Progressive Era attempt to embrace knowledge as society sought to impose order over life. Kizer was well suited for this role, having

Seen here from left to right are Catherine Baltz and her daughters Anna and Lena. Birdie Kizer stands between the daughters.

grown up and spent his youth on the family farm. He had a reputation for caring for sick animals, spending hours caring for a sick cow, horse or pig. At the age of twenty-five, he began working as a veterinarian. At the time, this required no formal training or education, and no licensure was needed. In fact, Arkansas did not formalize requirements for a veterinarian license until 1915, when it enacted new laws as part of the Progressive push for order. Like others, Kizer was grandfathered in and able to continue practicing.[46]

The Kizers' service as county agents even predated the creation of the extension service. In 1910, John Kizer listed his occupation as a special agent with the U.S. Department of Agriculture. In 1920, the couple resided on Jordan Street in Pocahontas, near the stately homes that lined Thomasville Avenue. John and Birdie had been married for eighteen years and, by all appearances, were doing well financially. According to the 1920 census, John still considered himself a farmer, worked as a veterinarian and served as the county agent. The Kizers' home had no mortgage, and the couple had no other debt. This would soon change. Kizer began amassing significant debt, invested heavily in the stock market and saw many family members and friends die, challenging the rules of coincidence.

3

MALARIA

Geography and environmental conditions were critical regarding disease and residents' health in eastern Arkansas. As previously stated, Pocahontas and Randolph County straddle two of Arkansas's unique geographical divisions, the Ozarks and the Delta. Early settlers associated the swamps of the bottomlands of the Delta, along with their often putrid smells, with sickness. They often referred to the "bad air" of these areas and sought to avoid such places, especially in the summer. This sickness was often labeled "ague," and symptoms included fever, chills, headaches, body aches, nausea, vomiting and diarrhea. Untreated patients could become anemic and experience liver failure, kidney failure and death. Ague later became known as malaria.[47]

Death was a fact of life in settler communities such as Randolph County. This attitude of accepting fate continued even after the region was no longer a wilderness of the frontier. In part, this attitude can be attributed to the state of medical care in communities like Pocahontas. While the region had a sizable number of doctors—even communities like Pitman and Ravenden Springs boasted doctors—the medical care was far from advanced. It was not uncommon for rural residents to live and die without seeing a doctor. Deaths from sickness, as viruses were often known, were not unusual and were seen as a normal part of life. It is worth noting that at this time many children died within the first couple of years.

Malaria caused significant suffering in eastern and central Arkansas. Mosquitoes most often spread the infectious disease transmitted by the plasmodium parasite. The infection typically began ten to fifteen days after being bitten by a mosquito carrying the parasite. Those patients lucky enough to recover could look forward to recurrences of the disease months and years later, as well as lasting side effects. Malaria is not native to North America. The disease is native to tropical climates such as portions of Africa, Asia and Latin America. During the classical Roman era, it was often called "Roman fever," and the Romans, like Arkansans, associated the infection with swamps and lousy air.[48]

Malaria is often seen as a negative side effect of European conquest and exploration, also known as the Columbian Exchange. Spanish explorer Hernando de Soto and his men became the first Europeans to set foot in present-day Arkansas in 1541, though it is worth noting that there is no evidence de Soto passed through present-day Randolph County. Historians have long argued that these Spanish men of fortune brought foreign biological agents and diseases that quickly spread among the native population, devastating whole groups and leading to the depopulation of the region that later explorers would make note of. Historians agree that de Soto and others introduced diseases like smallpox that devastated Native Americans. Malaria cases increased in Arkansas and elsewhere in the South as the extent of African slavery expanded. Early visitors to Arkansas often documented malaria outbreaks in places such as the *Arkansas Post*, though most attacks occurred in the state's eastern region. Visitors and newcomers were particularly susceptible to the disease.[49]

Early settlers often noted the swarms of mosquitoes and took precautions, such as using mosquito netting, to combat the pesky insect. Malaria-related deaths ranked among the leading causes of death in many regions of the South, such as eastern Arkansas. Malaria also impacted the economy due to lost work time and productivity. Mosquitoes could not be avoided; swarms were common in the bottomland where the most fertile soil was found. These insects and the wealth derived from growing cotton and other crops went hand in hand. Most homes, even those of the more affluent, did not have screens on their windows. In many ways, this led the population to accept the disease as a given—deaths due to malaria were a fact of life.

Randolph County's geographic location meant that the eastern portions of the county—the bottomland across the Black River from

Pocahontas—were highly susceptible to malaria, while most of the county—the hills—was not. This fact led to the growth of some communities in the county, such as Ravenden Springs, Dalton and Maynard. Ravenden Springs developed as a health resort in the hills of western Randolph County and boasted several hotels. Maynard boasted a private academy in northern Randolph County, the Abbot Academy, or the Ouachita Academy. This private school provided dormitories for young women, while male students often boarded with local families. This school was part of a series of "Mountain Schools" established in the Ozark foothills to provide education during an era of limited public education. The Abbot Academy took advantage of its proximity to the Delta region by advertising that the school was far enough away from the swamps of eastern Arkansas to avoid sickness. This advertising strategy indicates that parents and students alike were concerned enough about the prospect of their sons and daughters contracting malaria that the location of their school, far from the regions associated with the disease, was important.[50]

While many early settlers and others associated mosquitoes with malaria, at least on some level, the connection would be confirmed only in the 1880s. This discovery was made near Pocahontas. In 1882, Dr. Zaphney Orto, a doctor in Walnut Ridge, the county seat of Lawrence County, provided proof that mosquitoes transmitted malaria. This evidence led to increased funding to study malaria and other diseases. National groups such as the Public Health Service and the Rockefeller Foundation poured financial resources into the fight. Local communities responded by draining swamps and sloughs to reduce the number of mosquitoes and thereby reduce the frequency of cases. These efforts led to significant success in some areas of Arkansas. Local and state leaders urged homeowners to invest in window screens and screen doors to limit mosquito exposure. While some of these measures were undertaken in Randolph County, they were not pursued on a large scale, and the number of insects did not diminish significantly.[51]

According to Dr. Ken Bridges, malaria rates remained high in Arkansas during the 1920s and '30s. Arkansas led the nation when it came to cases of malaria. Malaria would play a significant role in the John R. Kizer story, and the fact that the state suffered disproportionately from the disease meant that few people questioned a diagnosis of malaria in Randolph County in the 1920s and '30s.[52]

People at that time were more willing to accept a fatalistic attitude concerning sickness and death. While Pocahontas and rural Randolph County had many physicians, medical care was not advanced, even in places like Pitman, Maynard and Ravenden Springs. Death and untreatable sickness had been a part of Arkansas for some time, and people were conditioned to live with a certain degree of acceptance.

4

FIRST MURDERS

On careful examination of Morehead's "They Died Like Dogs," which appeared in the April 1957 edition of *True Detective*, it quickly becomes evident that the timeline for the incredible crimes that took place is problematic. Morehead claims that Kizer "underwent the incredible metamorphosis which stayed with him until the day he died." According to Morehead, after eight years of marriage, Kizer convinced Birdie to purchase a life insurance policy. They had been married for much longer. Morehead paints a picture of a man overcome with greed or the "love of money," as he puts it, who was willing to poison his wife to collect an insurance payout. Also troubling is that Morehead states that the death of Birdie was Kizer's first killing. This is not substantiated by a review of death records, tombstones or later reports about Kizer.[53]

Little to nothing is known about the source material used by Morehead. No records have been found indicating he visited Pocahontas. More than likely, he encountered an individual with limited knowledge of the crimes and built on the account to write a compelling story that he then sold to *True Detective*. In other words, he started with a grain of truth and developed a somewhat fictional tale around the meager facts he possessed. Interestingly, research has shown no examples of locals criticizing or questioning this account after it was published. Several questions still need to be answered. First, how widespread was the readership of *True Detective*? If it was limited, few people in the region may have even seen or read the story. Second, at some point, the story became known in Pocahontas. Why did no one question its falsehoods?

According to Morehead, the second murder associated with Kizer was that of Elmer Anderson. According to the account in *True Detective*, following the death of Birdie, Kizer began looking for a new wife. He allegedly took an interest in Martha Anderson. Anderson and her husband, Elmer, reportedly owned a substantial cattle farm north of Pocahontas. Morehead places the Anderson farm some thirty miles north of Pocahontas. This location means the farm more than likely would have been in Missouri. Morehead provides no source materials for "They Died Like Dogs," so researching the Andersons and other victims is no easy task. Allegedly, Martha Anderson traveled to Pocahontas on a shopping trip. Reportedly, this visit did not go unnoticed by Kizer, and he saw an opportunity. He loaded up his car and drove off toward the Anderson farm. Martha's return was delayed due to poor weather, and she stayed with friends in Pocahontas. Meanwhile, Kizer arrived at the farm during a thunderstorm, and Elmer Anderson offered to allow him to spend the night. Morehead provides no detail concerning what transpired between Kizer and Anderson that evening but alleges that the following morning, Anderson was dead.[54]

Here the story takes an exciting turn that, again, does not fit the historical facts of the day. On finding that Elmer Anderson had passed away overnight, Kizer reportedly called the local undertaker, Herman McNabb. In 1926, local phone service, while relatively new, was available in parts of the region. For instance, Maynard and Pocahontas each had a telephone exchange, and an exchange operated in the Pitman and Supply area. Phoning a neighbor was possible, but calls between Maynard and Pocahontas would only be possible for a few years. No telephone lines connected the multiple exchanges in the area. Suppose the Anderson farm was located thirty miles north of Pocahontas, as Morehead claims. In that case, there is almost no likelihood that Kizer or anyone else could have called Maynard or Pocahontas.[55]

Until 1926, the undertaker, McNabb, lived in Maynard, where he worked as a banker. In 1926, he relocated to Pocahontas, where he and Alf Lewis created a business partnership, creating a mortuary and a furniture store. Within a few years, McNabb and his wife, Nelle, became the sole owners of the funeral home business, while Lewis became the furniture store owner. McNabb would become a central figure in the John R. Kizer story.[56]

The death of Elmer Anderson cannot be substantiated, despite a careful examination of U.S. Census records for Randolph and Sharp County, Arkansas, or Ripley County, Missouri. No Elmer Anderson appears in 1900, 1910, 1920 or 1930 census records. Furthermore, no obituary for Elmer Anderson has been located.[57]

The possibility exists that Morehead changed the name of the victim. He admits that he changed at least one name in the article. Another possibility exists. The death of Elmer Anderson may be pure fiction. It has been proven that Morehead's claim that Birdie Kizer was the first victim is false. No Anderson is listed as a victim in the press accounts of Kizer's misdeeds. A methodical examination of obituaries in the *Pocahontas Star Herald* reveals only one obituary from 1926 that might match any portion of Morehead's description.[58]

> *Obituary of Robert Edwin Anderson*
> *Robert Edwin Anderson, died Saturday at his home 3 miles north of Pocahontas following a stroke of apoplexy. He was engaged in —— at home and Mrs. Anderson had come to town to do some shopping. Upon her return home, she found her husband setting in a chair at the kitchen table, unconscious. He died from —— later without having regained consciousness.*
>
> *The funeral was held Monday afternoon and internment was made in Masonic Cemetery. Rev. W.E. Hall, pastor of the Methodist church here, conducted the funeral service.*[59]
>
> *He is survived by the widow and two daughters, Mrs. Helen Kerley of McDongal and Mrs. Katie Pultzer of Newport; two brothers, A.M. Anderson of Hillsboro, Ill. And J.P. Anderson of Poplar Bluff, Mo and one sister Mrs. Story B. English of DeQueen, Ill.*

It is worth noting that Anderson's wife was Martha, though there seems to be no definitive evidence linking Kizer to Mr. Anderson's stroke and eventual death.[60]

Morehead claims that Kizer's second victim was none other than his own niece, Katie. She was the daughter of Kizer's older brother Julian. Katie was born in 1893 and married William F. (Finis) Riggs on March 5, 1927. Riggs was twenty-seven years Katie's senior. Finis Riggs was born on June 8, 1864, and made his living as a farmer. The Riggs family members were natives of Kentucky. Based on the 1900 U.S. Census, he rented his land, though he may have owned some land. Finis was listed as the head of his household and married to Mary E. Riggs. Finis and Mary Riggs appear to have had ten children; they divorced in February 1924. The only documentation of this divorce is found in a database of Arkansas divorces from 1923 to 1972. No reason for the divorce is provided, and no additional information has been found. What is known is that Finis Riggs married Katie Kizer on March 5, 1924, one month after his divorce was finalized. He and Katie had two children, a son and a daughter.[61]

In the Morehead account, Katie Riggs, John's niece, became ill, prompting Kizer to visit with groceries and his trusty medical bag. The Riggses welcomed "Uncle John" and even provided him with their spare room so he could look after his niece. Morehead quotes Kizer: "I'm all alone in the world. It doesn't matter where I live. I'm going to stay right here until my niece gets well. You have the farm to look after, Bob. You'll be busy. I can stay here and look after your wife." Morehead provides no citations for the quote. It should be pointed out that Kizer was not "alone in the world" at the time, as his wife, Birdie, was still alive. A second quote is used by Morehead: "Doctors are hopelessly old fashioned; I've got some stuff in my bag which will cure you in no time. You've only got a touch of malaria." This quote also has no citation, so there is no way to confirm the story.[62]

According to Morehead, Katie Riggs became John Kizer's third victim. In reality, John Riggs did not kill his niece. Katie lived to be sixty-nine years old. Following the death of Finis Riggs, she remarried and eventually moved to Tulsa, Oklahoma. Since Morehead clearly claims Kizer murdered the wife of Finis Riggs, it is worth noting that Mary Elizabeth Riggs, his first wife, passed away on February 27, 1933. Neither Mrs. Riggses death is associated with John Kizer, as Morehead asserts.[63]

5

FINANCIAL RUIN

It is often assumed that Black Tuesday, October 29, 1929, had little immediate effect on rural locales such as Pocahontas, Arkansas. The U.S. Stock Market crash followed the collapse of the London Stock Exchange in September and is often seen as the beginning of the Great Depression. While this is an oversimplification, the crash did signal a worsening global economy and an intensification of economic problems across the United States. The economy had soured during the Roaring Twenties following the First World War. Much of this decade of prosperity was built on an inequitable economy that was impossible to sustain. Much of the economy was based on the automobile and construction industries. Once these sectors began to fail, the rest of the economic house of cards soon fell. The 1920s also saw average Americans and financial institutions participate in rampant speculation with little governmental oversight. When the market crashed, significant investors were ruined; many small investors suffered as well.[64]

In many ways, the Great Depression and the effects of the stock market crash were slow to emerge in Arkansas. The state lagged behind economically in the years before the Depression, and conditions would only get worse following the events of October 1929. For instance, farm wages in Arkansas were only about half of those in other states. In 1929, the average Arkansas farmworker earned $1.65 per day.[65]

In other ways, the Great Depression in Arkansas continued the bad luck and poor planning that had plagued it since statehood. In 1836, Arkansas ratified a constitution that allowed the state to charter two banks. Before statehood,

Arkansas had no financial institutions, which hampered its economic development and efforts to attract settlers. The state did not own the two banks, but they were backed by the state. This system left the Arkansas State Bank and the Arkansas Real Estate Bank susceptible to corruption. In fact, a debate in the first session of the Arkansas General Assembly led the House Speaker to murder the Randolph County representative on the chamber floor. Once these banks failed, the state held much of the debt. This debt was not paid through a series of questionable deals and ended up in the hands of others, who sought payment from Arkansas. The state had also suffered immensely during the Civil War and its aftermath. Reconstruction brought about a more liberal, democratic constitution, but it did not last long. In 1874, Redeemers drafted and ratified a limited constitution that forbade the state from spending freely while limiting the powers of the governor and the state government. All the while, the growing debt hung over the state's head. Arkansas essentially operated on a cash basis, which crippled its ability to pursue economic growth and fully participate in the New South and Progressive Eras. When the Great Mississippi River Flood took place, the state was in a dire position and unable to help its citizens effectively. Arkansas had not yet recovered from the flood when the Great Depression hit.

Arkansas suffered in unique ways during the Depression. The state's per capita income was the lowest in the nation. Half of its citizens were unemployed, and many lost their property due to delinquent property taxes. The state's economy was dependent on cotton, which sold for six cents a pound in 1931. Thousands of Arkansans lost what little money they had when more than two hundred banks failed. While the state benefited from President Franklin Roosevelt's policies and his New Deal programs, not all Arkansans were happy about these policies. Some conservative Arkansas elites, mainly members of the business community and the planter class, opposed the New Deal while taking advantage of the programs. These men, such as Robert E. Lee Wilson of Mississippi County, profited from the New Deal while politically opposing Roosevelt and his allies in the state. In 1932, Arkansans elected Junius Marion Futrell as governor. He had been a judge and a state senator from Greene County. Futrell ran with the full backing of the state's planter elite. He pursued policies of retrenchment. He closed public schools, cut spending and opposed many New Deal programs because they were liberal. For example, Futrell wanted to end public high schools in the state. During his administration, voters approved the Nineteenth Amendment to the state constitution, which required a three-fourths majority to raise taxes. The residents of Arkansas once again voted against their self-interest. Futrell was supported by the planter elite that Kizer so desired to become part of, though he never fully achieved this status. Futrell's policies hampered Arkansas's ability to survive the Great Depression and often made conditions worse than they had to be, in the name of conservatism. Arkansas responded to the Depression the way it had to so many other turning points in its history: poorly. The state paid the price for years to come.[66]

Following the stock market crash, Arkansas experienced a drought that affected the state's agricultural economy. The twin economic and environmental disasters were more than many Arkansans could sustain. John Kizer had always sought to join the ranks of the local rural elites. He had profited tremendously during the Roaring Twenties, like many of his peers. The number of mercantile houses, hotels, banks and fine homes was a testament to Pocahontas's full participation in the decade of excess. Kizer was not immune. For many years, he had been investing in farm acreage and city lots. By 1929, Kizer had amassed significant land and a fine home on Jordan Street in Pocahontas. Like many other Americans of his day, Kizer began investing in the market and "borrowed heavily" to purchase stock in hopes of reaping significant financial gain. This debt placed Kizer, like many Americans, in a precarious financial position and made him highly susceptible to the crash. The crash of 1929 triggered a slow-rolling financial ruin from which John Kizer would never emerge. The stock market crash and the economic decline cost him $80,000 between 1929 and 1930. When adjusted for today's currency, Kizer lost $1,412,000. This was devastating to a man who had grown up poor and spent his life working to attain economic and social status.[67]

Kizer, like many investors during the Roaring Twenties, tended to be heavily involved in speculation. During this era, it was not uncommon for investors like Kizer to put their savings in the market, mortgage land and use the equity to invest or purchase stocks on the margin, using real estate and other investments as collateral. John Kizer invested his savings, and as his investments rose, he sought to raise considerable sums of capital to support the ever-climbing stock market. Kizer, like many Americans, turned to local banks to raise money. Over the years, Kizer had slowly added to his property portfolio and, at one time, owed almost nothing. This portfolio became an easy means to raise revenue, which he then invested in the market. He more than likely borrowed heavily from local banks, though no banking records have been found to substantiate how much debt Kizer accumulated during the period. The *St. Louis Post-Dispatch* and other publications were able to document his losses in the later investigation.[68]

Randolph County and Pocahontas fully participated in the Roaring Twenties. One way this participation is evident is in the number of financial institutions or banks that operated in the county before the Great Depression. In 1903, the Bank of Biggers was established with thirty-six incorporators. Within a few short years, three banks had been chartered in Pocahontas. These were the Randolph County Bank, the Pocahontas State Bank and the First National Bank. Eventually, these three banks merged to form the Randolph State Bank. This institution, like some 30 percent of banks in existence in 1929, did not survive the Depression. John Kizer lost a considerable amount of money in this bank failure. This event left Pocahontas with no financial institution. In 1931, the Bank of Biggers stockholders agreed to consolidate their institution with the State Bank of Success, founded in 1919, to form a new bank, the Bank of Pocahontas. Each bank agreed to supply $25,000 in capital and $2,500 in surplus funds. The latest Bank of Pocahontas opened for business on March 2, 1931. The State Bank of Success surrendered its charter, and the new bank operated under the Bank of Biggers charter. The institution opened in the Guaranty Building on the north side of Pocahontas Square, ending months with no banking facilities in Pocahontas.[69]

It is impossible to know if John Kizer murdered William Finis Riggs, though, in retrospect, it is easy to assume that Riggs was his first victim. If Kizer did murder his niece's husband, many questions remain. Why did he do it? How did he do it? Why did someone who was by all accounts a happily married man and an upstanding member of the community murder a family member? And how did he keep this knowledge from his wife?

6

BIRDIE

John and Birdie Kizer built a successful life together. Seen from the outside, the Kizers were a model family that fully embraced the Progressive Era. They both worked as county extension agents for a time, and then John Kizer devoted himself full-time to his veterinarian practice. Birdie was exceptionally well thought of in the community. She was kind, compassionate and caring. Birdie was especially popular with those who relied on classes she taught as a county agent. She taught the latest techniques in canning, food preservation and housekeeping skills to women of all social and economic types. John bred and raised hogs and cattle. He ran newspaper advertisements across the region touting his livestock for sale. At times, he also raised chickens and sold them.[70]

John and Birdie, by all appearances, were doing well financially. According to the 1920 U.S. Census, John still considered himself a farmer. He also worked as a veterinarian and served as the county agent. The Kizer home had no mortgage, and the couple appears to have had no debt. They seemed devoted to each other. Throughout his life, John sought respectability and economic and social standing. At first, Birdie was an asset when it came to achieving these goals, but before long, John grew envious of his wife's popularity and realized she was much better liked than he was. This realization alarmed John, as he cared passingly about what people thought and said about him. Professionally, he was well regarded, but on a personal level, John was not well liked. He was considered cheap by many in the community. He often refused to give to charity or to good causes. John was considered a miser by many, and along with his well-known dislike for dogs, many citizens of Randolph County were suspicious of him. After all, who hates dogs? His callous disregard for life bothered many in the community.[71]

In 1927, John and Birdie Kizer had been married for ten years. By all appearances, these had been happy years, as John moved from working as the county agent to devoting more time to his veterinarian practice. He had also begun purchasing land, often at tax auctions on the courthouse steps. In many ways, John viewed the accumulation of land as the ultimate status symbol. After all, no one is making any more land. In fact, John became obsessed with building his real estate portfolio. He seemed adept at picking up parcels of land for bargain prices and, during the 1920s, carried little to no debt. The couple's wealth grew significantly in these years as they fully participated in the Roaring Twenties. They owned an automobile, had a lovely home and traveled among Pocahontas's upper crust.[72]

Birdie had three children by her first marriage. The children lived with the Kizers for periods, but by 1927, the children were grown and gone from home, leaving Birdie and John as empty nesters. According to the 1920 U.S. Census, the Kizer household consisted of just John and Birdie.[73]

In 1957, Charles Morehead published what became a widely read version of the John Kizer story, "They Died Like Dogs," in *True Detective*. Morehead's account of the John Kizer murders defined the gruesome events associated with the veterinarian who hated dogs. As is often the case, the story of John Kizer became the stuff of legend. By 1957, the story had been told repeatedly and embellished. For example, Morehead wrote, "It wasn't until 1925, when John Kizer had been married for 8 years, that he underwent the incredible metamorphosis which was to stay with him until the day he died." The couple had been married for much longer. Morehead claimed that Kizer urged Birdie to take out a life insurance policy in 1925. But Birdie Kizer's obituary in the *Pocahontas Star Herald* clearly states that she died in December 1927, not in 1925. The couple had been married for longer than eight years at the time as well.[74]

Birdie Kizer, by all accounts, was devoted to John. At the urging of her husband, Birdie purchased a life insurance policy in 1927. Soon she began to complain of feeling unwell. Birdie had no energy; she suffered from body aches and joint pain. She suffered from convulsions and ran a high fever. These symptoms began after John inoculated his wife for the dreaded malaria. As his wife grew more sick, John appeared to be only moderately alarmed. While he did notify Birdie's adult children that their mother was ill, he assured his stepchildren that there was little to worry about. After all, he had cured numerous animals. The children urged their stepfather to take their mother to a doctor, but Kizer refused.[75]

For one thing, he argued that there was no use in paying a doctor when he had all the medicines he could possibly need. A more sinister reason lay behind his refusal to take his wife to the doctor. He feared that a reputable doctor would discover that Birdie Kizer was being poisoned.[76]

Birdie grew weaker and weaker as the days passed. Her children were alarmed, but their stepfather was trying to keep them away. The veterinarian was treating his wife with a small arsenal of drugs that he kept in his bag, but none of these seemed to be doing the trick. For the most part, Kizer remained by her side, tending to his sick wife day and night. On rare occasions, he did leave home to treat a sick animal, but not often. One day when Kizer left home, Birdie's son came to visit. He had been waiting on Kizer to go. What he saw disturbed him. His mother was wasting away. She looked horrible and appeared to be frail. He loaded his mother into his car and took her to a local doctor.[77]

Morehead indicates that Birdie was taken to the local hospital. Due to their stepfather's economic and social position, the children took their mother to St. Bernard's Hospital in July 1900. The hospital grew out of an effort by the local Olivetan Benedictine Sisters to care for the people of Northeast Arkansas during a malaria epidemic. The facility began with just six rooms, but by 1923, the hospital had expanded to a sixty-bed facility.[78]

In the 1920s, Pocahontas, like the rest of Northeast Arkansas, had no hospital and would not for many years. Roads in this region were rough, and Birdie's journey to St. Bernard's could not have been pleasant. The drastic step of taking their mother to the hospital demonstrates how serious her children thought the situation was. Other factors may have contributed as well. For instance, Birdie's children were likely unsure if they could trust local doctors who had professional relationships with John Kizer. By traveling forty-four miles, they were also putting space between their mother and their stepfather, signifying that they were at the very least upset that he had not taken their mother to the doctor and, at the most, suspicious that John was responsible for Birdie's illness. The doctor—or doctors, as Morehead suggests—examined Birdie and discovered that her right arm was severely swollen. These physicians found the site where her husband had been injecting her with small doses of poison. Kizer used small amounts so that, over time, the poison would build up in his wife's body. In the meantime, this poisoning's symptoms resembled those of malaria. Birdie's arm was so damaged by the poison that the doctor argued the only hope was to amputate the arm. The injection site had become so swollen and damaged that there was little hope of saving the arm. The doctors worked diligently to save Birdie Kizer's life, but she died two weeks after her arm was amputated. Kizer had stonewalled her children until he had injected their mother with enough poison to be terminal. Her death was slow and painful.[79]

Birdie Kizer passed away at St. Bernard's on Thursday, December 22, 1927, two weeks after the amputation of her right arm. John moved quickly to have the funeral. McNabb Funeral Home was paid to promptly transport her body back to Pocahontas, and a funeral was hastily arranged for the following day. Kizer had been at odds with his stepchildren since before they took their mother to the hospital against his will. While Kizer was successful when it came to a speedy funeral, the children overruled him when it came to the funeral location. While John Kizer never professed deep spiritual beliefs, he desperately wanted to be part of Pocahontas's social elite. For Kizer, this meant being affiliated with the Pocahontas Methodist Church. Birdie, on the other hand, had been affiliated with the First Church of Christ. Her children insisted her funeral be held at her church, with Reverend J. Will Henley and Reverend W.E. Hall officiating. She was buried in the Pocahontas Masonic Cemetery. According to the *Pocahontas Star Herald*, the funeral was attended by a huge crowd consisting of many out-of-town guests. Birdie had been an active member of the Red Cross Chapter No. 40, and her sisters showed up in record numbers to pay their respects. According to her obituary, she was survived by her husband, John R. Kizer; one son, Jim Brooks of Little Rock; and two daughters, Mrs. Essie Dunham of McAlester, Oklahoma, and Mrs. Lorine Fisher of Walnut Ridge.[80]

Birdie's children were shocked by her sudden death. After all, she had been a vibrant woman much loved by the community and her children. No records exist to illuminate the relationship between stepfather and children, but John Kizer had been married to their mother for many years. The children had grown up in the Kizer home before marrying and starting their own families. Due to the circumstances surrounding their mother's death, the children had questions and sought answers.

Morehead's account alleged that Essie, Birdie's youngest daughter, blamed Kizer for her mother's death and quickly left home and got married following the funeral. Once again, Morehead's facts are questionable. In fact, the three Brooks children were already grown and had left the Kizer home at the time of their mother's death. Jim Brooks lived in Little Rock, while his sister Lorine Fisher was married and lived in Walnut Ridge. Lorine and her husband owned an insurance and real estate business. At one time, the Fisher Insurance Agency had been part of Lantie Martin's Martin Agency in Pocahontas. Birdie's second daughter, Essie Dunham, lived in McAlester, Oklahoma, with her husband at the time of her mother's death.[81]

It has always been assumed that financial gain was the motive for the murder of Birdie Kizer. In the Morehead account of the killings, it is alleged that John Kizer had urged his wife to purchase an insurance policy. In 1936, the *St. Louis Post-Dispatch*, which did the most in-depth reporting on the crimes of John Kizer, found no concrete proof that he had profited from the death of Birdie. Financial moves by Kizer following her death provide some evidence, though not conclusive, that he had more money to spend. Remember, Kizer was not known to freely spend money, nor was he prone to donate to charity. Following Birdie's death, he made at least one conspicuous purchase. Kizer donated an elaborate stained-glass window to the Pocahontas Methodist Church, where he had wanted Birdie's funeral. Birdie's name appeared on one side of the window; the other had Kizer's name and those of his stepchildren.[82]

If greed was the central motivation for this murder, as has long been the accepted case, why would Kizer need money in late 1927? One strong possibility is rooted in one of the worst natural disasters that ever occurred in the region. The flood of 1927, sometimes referred to as the Great Mississippi River Flood, proved to be not only destructive but also costly. While the states of the Mississippi Delta were affected by the flood, Arkansas suffered more than other states in the region, according to historian Nancy Hendricks. John Kizer had few if any holdings in the affected areas of the Black River bottoms. The financial ruin that arrived with the floods dramatically affected his business. If this business downturn was severe enough, he needed an infusion of cash to stay financially afloat.[83]

Kizer does not appear to have married Birdie to murder her and collect life insurance. In this instance, he decided, after many years, to murder his wife. In any case, Kizer appears to have a type regarding women. Like his next wife, Birdie was no widow, as Morehead claimed, but rather a divorcée who had fled a troubled marriage. Kizer may have seen these women as needing him, or he may have seen them as damaged and, therefore, easy to control. The case of Mrs. Anderson is more than likely contrived to help Morehead make his point that Kizer sought to marry a wealthy widow, which we now know is not valid. More than likely, Kizer sought out women he thought he could easily manipulate. A strong woman like Mrs. Anderson certainly does not fit this mold.

ROSENA

John Kizer wasted no time finding the next Mrs. John Kizer. Shortly after the death of Birdie, he met Rosena Arnold. Rosena was the daughter of William F. Bonner and his wife, Mary E. Brown, who lived just outside Pocahontas. William Bonner was born in Little Rock and had resided in Jackson County before moving to Randolph County. Rosena graduated from Pocahontas High School and briefly attended the University of Arkansas in Fayetteville. In 1919, Rosena married Lundie Thomas Arnold in Poplar Bluff, Missouri. Arnold was a thirty-six-year-old farmer who owned much land in Lawrence and Jackson Counties in Arkansas. Rosena was ten years younger than her husband. In August 1920, she gave birth to a son, Bonner. At the time, the couple was living in Swifton in Jackson County.[84]

Morehead describes Rosena as a widow and the "richest woman Kizer had yet dealt with." According to the Morehead version of the story, she inherited several blocks of real estate, farmland and other property when Lundie died in November 1928. In fact, Lundie had died in 1928, but he left Rosena no land. Rosena Arnold had sued for divorce in December 1927 in Randolph County. She took Bonner and moved in with her parents when her marriage fell apart. When Arnold passed away, young Bonner became his sole heir, but Bonner could not manage his property, since he was a minor. Rosena acted as trustee until Bonner came of age and could control his affairs.

Kizer's interest in Rosena was largely because she was a divorcée with a child. While divorce had become more acceptable and attainable by this time, it did not mean that a divorced woman with a child would have an easy life. In Rosena's case, she was highly dependent on her parents following her divorce. In Rosena, Kizer saw a woman who would need him, be committed to him and be dependent on him. The last sort of wife John Kizer wanted was an independent woman who spoke her mind.

William Bonner owned a successful farming operation north of Pocahontas. The Bonner home has been described as "luxurious." They owned farmland as well as property in Pocahontas. He knew John Kizer and, from time to time, used the veterinarian's services. Kizer may have met Rosena on one of these visits, or they may have been introduced by friends in town. In any case, they began to court or date. The couple was married at 7:00 p.m. on Monday, March 25, 1929, in a simple service. Morehead described the wedding as lavish, claiming that the grandeur of the ceremony shocked many of those in attendance. This differs from accounts of the time. According to the *Pocahontas Star Herald*, the couple embarked on a short honeymoon following the wedding. They first traveled to Paragould in Greene County before going to Doniphan in Ripley County, Missouri, Newport and then Batesville before returning home.[85]

Little is known about Kizer's marriage. Rosena and her son, Bonner, moved into Kizer's spacious home at 507 Kizer Avenue in South Pocahontas. Kizer purchased new furniture and one of the first electric refrigerators in Pocahontas for his new bride. Based on outward appearances, Kizer relished the role of stepdad to Bonner. Rosena's parents liked and respected Kizer and hoped for the best after their daughter failed her first marriage. The divorce had left Rosena little, though following her ex-husband's death, Bonner stood to inherit substantial land in Lawrence and Jackson Counties when he came of age.[86]

Kizer married Rosena in March 1929, and the first few months of the marriage seemed good. On September 16, 1929, Rosena died after a short illness. People in the community were shocked; they thought of poor Bonner and John. How could any man have such bad luck to have lost two wives in such a short amount of time? Here a critical pattern emerges concerning the two women John Kizer married. Both married Kizer following marriages that ended in divorce. Divorce, while easier to obtain by the 1920s, remained uncommon. The fact that both women who married John Kizer were divorced could mean he had a "type" or sought out women whom previous relationships had hurt. These women may have been more receptive to his advances and charms. For instance, he seems to have been devoted to both wives initially. In the case of Birdie, he provided her with a home, greater respectability and a social position. While Birdie surpassed her husband and was much better liked, he offered her access to a new social world. In the case of Rosena, the marriage lasted a short five months, but during that time, he showered her with goods and provided a lovely home for her and her son.[87]

The death of Rosena Kizer mirrored that of Birdie in many ways. The events leading up to her death remain vague. Morehead takes significant liberties with the account of her death. For example, according to Morehead, Rosena's death came about in 1932, three years after her actual death. The *St. Louis Post-Dispatch* reported that Kizer collected $33,000 in life insurance following his wife's death. In "They Died Like Dogs," Morehead provides significant information about this insurance policy and how it came about. In this narrative, Kizer urges Rosena to purchase life insurance. He argues that the policy would take care of Bonner if anything happened to them. According to Morehead, the couple has a significant disagreement concerning insurance. Rosena appears to oppose life insurance, and her father is equally opposed. This story is unsubstantiated and should be treated with suspicion due to its many problems.[88]

On the other hand, a few elements of this story stand out. For one thing, Rosena supposedly said that she had enough money to take care of Bonner. However, she appears to have retained little in the way of finances following her first marriage. Morehead indicates that Rosena said that Bonner had sufficient assets, meaning that life insurance would not be necessary. This claim is factual as far as it goes. Bonner was the sole heir to his father's substantial estate and would be well off when he became an adult.

What is known is that John Kizer collected $33,000 when Rosena died. She died just before the stock market crash, and it is reasonable to believe that he invested this money in the raging market, only to suffer substantial losses just weeks later. The fact that Kizer had murdered two wives and raised little to no suspicion fueled his greed and desire for money. Many questions remain, and any discussion of motive should include a discussion of mental illness. While the United States made strides during the Progressive Era and the Roaring Twenties, mental healthcare was not among them. Therapy was unheard of, and most people who suffered from depression, anxiety or other mental health problems had almost no resources. Whether Kizer's problems were rooted in mental illness or pure greed, he had stumbled on to a profitable formula.[89]

The *St. Louis Post-Dispatch* reported Rosena Kizer dying from convulsions. Reports indicate that Kizer and his wife drove to Hardy in neighboring

Sharp County to purchase goats. Apparently, Rosena began feeling ill on the trip. Kizer had been inoculating Rosena against malaria, just as he had with Birdie. The couple spent two days in Hardy, and when she returned, she was pretty ill. She complained of painful cramping and body aches. Once home, Rosena went to bed, and Kizer, as he had with his first wife, resisted calling a doctor. Morehead claims that Kizer eventually called for a doctor, but no other evidence of this house call has been found. Rosena never recovered.[90]

Following the death of his wife, Kizer, as he had with Riggs, Birdie and Anderson—if we are to believe that Kizer murdered him—arranged for a quick burial. The funeral was held on Tuesday, just one day after her death, at the Methodist church. The service was conducted by Reverends F.W. Varner, T.H. Sherrill and W.E. Hall. Once again, no autopsy was required, and no investigation took place. Kizer quickly produced two separate insurance policies valued at over $30,000 in all. Few questions were raised, and the insurance companies paid quickly.[91]

The fact that Kizer could arrange such quick burials following his murders should not necessarily shine a bad light on any local officials or on the local undertaker, McNabb. Most funerals took place quickly, though typically not as soon as those paid for by Kizer. While they should have raised more suspicion than they apparently did, all of the victims had died from what appeared to be natural causes. But it is easy to question why no mention or questions arose concerning swollen injection sites on multiple victims. No autopsy requirement existed then, and local officials seemed uninterested at best.

The ease with which Kizer disposed of Rosena spurred him to further action. In the Morehead account, he murders an elderly aunt, Lizzie Robinson, and her friend Willa Brown. Here Morehead may have changed the name of Kizer's aunt. According to the *Post-Dispatch*, the aunt in question is Sarah Stubblefield. Morehead admitted in his story that some names were changed to protect some individuals. Aunt Sarah passed away on July 29, 1932. She had been fighting off a cold when Kizer came to visit her. He assured her he could treat her and have her feeling better soon. He then gave her medicine. Unfortunately, she soon felt much worse, and according to newspaper reports, she told a visitor, "He's killed me," shortly before she died. Kizer did not have an insurance policy on his aunt, but he possessed $1,700 that belonged to her. He kept the money. Due to the quick nature of Aunt Sarah's death, Kizer called on his friend Dr. Loftis to sign the death certificate. This continued Kizer's practice of convincing a medical professional to sign off on the deaths to alleviate suspicions. Loftis agreed to sign the death certificate. Based on the investigative reporting of the day, Willa Brown was not murdered, and no record of this victim has been found. Kizer had enjoyed significant prosperity as a veterinarian, but nothing compared to what murder was producing. Four months later, he committed his next murder.[92]

No clues explain why he moved to murder Rosena so quickly following their marriage. One hypothesis is, simply, that he was driven by greed. Put another way, Kizer was desperate for money and saw killing his new wife as the quickest means to obtain it. While this is entirely plausible, another possibility exists. Rosena Kizer quickly proved far too independent and willing to speak her mind. If this was the case, it would have upset Kizer. He had fully expected her to be docile and easy to control. Kizer would have looked for a quick way out of the union. Divorce was out of the question as far as he was concerned, even though he could have protected most if not all of his property. A divorce would have severely damaged the careful image he had cultivated in the community.

MR. AND MRS. BONNER

Following Rosena's death, John Kizer continued to raise young Bonner. The boy seemed to like Kizer, and local accounts indicate the two were close. John and Bonner were brought closer by the death of their wife and mother, respectively. Bonner was also close to his grandparents William and Elizabeth Bonner. The Bonners lived north of Pocahontas in a substantial home. The Bonners did not suspect Kizer in the death of their daughter. They were too old to raise a child. After all, Bonner loved his stepfather, and the Bonners seemed content to let their grandson remain with Kizer. They went as far as to invite Kizer and Bonner to move to their farm to keep them company. The house on Kizer Avenue was closed, and the two moved north of town to care for the Bonners.[93]

When Kizer married Rosena, he knew that she was divorced. He also knew that she had little money to call her own. Following her divorce, she and Bonner lived with her parents until she married John Kizer. Kizer, though, also was well aware that Bonner Kizer was the sole heir to his father's substantial estate. This information put Rosena and her parents in a dangerous position. First, Rosena stood between Kizer and the wealth that Bonner inherited. Following her death, her parents stood in the way. It did not help matters that the Bonners themselves had substantial assets.[94]

Kizer was not content for very long in his in-laws' home. He soon began to push for the Bonners to join him and his son in Pocahontas. Shortly after Rosena's death, John Kizer adopted Bonner with her parents' blessing. The Bonners resisted moving to the Kizer house in town. Their home was excellent, and they did not wish to leave it. Finally, Kizer convinced them to move to Pocahontas temporarily for the winter. Soon the whole family—John, Bonner, William and Elizabeth—were living in John Kizer's home in Pocahontas.

With Rosena out of the way and Bonner officially adopted, John began formulating a plan. For his project to work, he needed more influence over the Bonners. As long as they had a lovely home to return to, he had no hope of getting his hands on their money and land. Soon after the Bonners moved to town, their house mysteriously burned in the middle of the night. The home was a total loss. Now Kizer had more control. The Bonners were thankful to have a home with Kizer and their grandson.[95]

While Kizer was highly interested in Bonner's inheritance, how much access he would have had to the assets is not known. Morehead contends that Kizer "bought stocks and bonds in the boy's name. He issued cash on local mortgages, making out the mortgages in Bonner's name." By this point, the stock market crash had set in motion the Great Depression. Banks failed, even banks in Pocahontas and Randolph County. Kizer's losses in the 1929 crash were substantial, so Bonner's inheritance may have offered some liquidity for Kizer. But it is doubtful he could have borrowed from these funds indefinitely without raising severe suspicion.[96]

During this time, he pressured the Bonners to swap land with him. This was something William Bonner was unwilling to do. His stubbornness was proving to be problematic for Kizer. William was in the way. In early November 1932, William F. Bonner collapsed while walking through one of his fields. Kizer was right there to help him. Kizer and William were alone and at some distance from the Bonner home. According to Kizer, William suffered a stroke. In the Morehead version of events, William Bonner did not die in 1932, but in 1934; again, the facts appear to have changed over time. Morehead argues that Kizer helped the old man back to the house and placed him in bed, then gave him a couple of capsules from his medical bag. William suffered extreme pain for two weeks before dying on November 11, 1932. Dr. Loftis agreed to sign the death certificate attesting that a stroke had killed Mr. Bonner, even though the physician had not examined the man before his death.[97]

Following a swift funeral arranged by William's devoted son-in-law, Elizabeth continued to live with Kizer and her grandson, Bonner. Soon after the funeral, Kizer submitted a life insurance policy that he had purchased on William Bonner. The $3,000 policy listed him as a co-beneficiary along with Mrs. Bonner. The Bonners had no knowledge that such a policy existed. It is not known what Rosena's sister Sylvia Holland thought about Kizer.[98]

For the next two years, Elizabeth, John and young Bonner lived in some state of tranquility, and no murders were attributed to Kizer. He had access to the Bonner money and control of the Arnold estate, at least to some degree. Some of this contentment can be attributed to the fact that no one challenged John's position until Bonner came of age and gained control over his inheritance. But the closer Bonner came to adulthood, the more Kizer worried. He saw a huge financial prize slipping from his grip.

Elizabeth Bonner served a purpose for Kizer. She helped him care for Bonner. Where her husband had proved reluctant to grant Kizer access to his best farmland, she was more than willing to deed much of it to her son-in-law. After all, the land would be Bonner's one day. Kizer moved slowly when it came to Elizabeth. Young Bonner was doing well in school, and he would not come of age and gain legal access to his inheritance for some time still. Kizer felt no need to rush. Elizabeth deeded much of her land to Kizer, but he still had to file the deeds. In fact, he wanted to keep from the public for as long as possible the knowledge that she had transferred him the land. Only after her death, which followed a short illness, did Kizer take the time to go to the Randolph County Courthouse and register the deeds. Elizabeth had conveyed to him 585 acres of prime farmland and several parcels of property in Pocahontas. The total value of the property she gave Kizer was well over $25,000. Today, this would be worth $500,000 or more. As these transactions became public knowledge, some questions were asked. Kizer pushed back, saying Bonner would inherit it all one day, so it only made sense for him to manage the property. After all, if things continued as they were, one day, Bonner would be a wealthy man. Not everyone was pleased with this answer. For example, Elizabeth Bonner's sister in St. Louis did not like it at all. While no one in Pocahontas seemed ready to call Kizer a murderer, some asked questions.

9

"LITTLE BONNER"

Bonner Kizer experienced more grief than most young men his age. By the time he turned sixteen, he had lost his father, mother and grandparents and found himself living with an adoptive father who had been married to his mother mere months before her death. Yet, despite these tragic events, the young man seems to have been well-adjusted. He was well-liked in the community, popular at Pocahontas High School and active at the local Methodist church.[99]

Bonner was also financially set for the future by most accounts. At his father's death, Bonner inherited a significant amount of property with which he could do as he pleased once he came of age. But even the most well-adjusted young man had to wonder about his future. Bonner loved John Kizer but also found the older man to be controlling. He respected his father and considered himself lucky that the man took him in to raise him following the death of his mother and grandparents, but he worried about the future and recognized that he had no family.[100]

As Bonner got older, he began to discuss his future with Kizer. What Kizer heard concerned him. The young man dreamed of traveling the world. This was not an unusual dream for a young man who had seldom left Randolph County. As he and Kizer began discussing his future, his father wanted him to finish high school and stay in Pocahontas. After all, he had a lot of property, and Kizer was there to help him manage his assets, just as he had helped Bonner's grandparents. Bonner had other ideas. He was fond of reading and gravitated to stories of world adventure. He wanted to join the U.S. Navy.

This alarmed his father. If the boy entered the navy, would he ever return to Pocahontas? What would become of his property? The boy went as far as to claim he wanted to make the navy a career. This further alarmed Kizer, who could see his control over a significant amount of land and its wealth slipping away. At first, this raised few concerns for Kizer, as the boy was only sixteen. But Bonner then started talking about dropping out of school and joining the navy. Kizer could not and would not allow this to happen. He needed a plan. The boy could not be allowed to quit school and join the navy. Kizer had to get his hands on that property. Seven years after the stock market crash, economic conditions were improving, but Kizer's finances never fully recovered. He had married Rosena Arnold believing she had more land and money than she did. Most people spoke of the young woman as a widow, but she had divorced her husband and moved with her young son back to Randolph County to live with her parents. She had little money and relied on her parents for support. Rosena saw Kizer, who was nearly twice her age, as a way out of a bad situation. He was well-established, appeared wealthy and seemed to make a good stepfather for her young son.[101]

Soon after their marriage, Kizer realized that any property and wealth was in trust for Rosena's son, Bonner. She could not spend it, and he could not get his hands on it. The marriage was only months old when Kizer killed Rosena and collected on an insurance policy. Kizer saw this marriage as a mistake or a misstep, and now he sought a way out of it that could provide the most financial gain. For several years, Kizer seems to have been content to raise Bonner but did not intend to let him leave town and build a life. The time had come for Kizer to cash in on all he had invested in the Bonners and get the ultimate payoff. After much thought, Kizer saw football as providing him with an opportunity, and he hoped no one would be the wiser when Bonner was gone.[102]

Bonner was small for his age but was a popular student at Pocahontas High School. Despite his small stature, he played football. The Pocahontas Redskins played Corning High School, one of their biggest rivals, on October 9, 1936. During the game, a couple of Corning Bobcat players appear to have picked out the smaller player for some rough attention. They tackled Bonner, driving their knees into his abdomen and shoulder. Bonner's shoulder was injured late in the game, forcing him to leave the field. Bonner had not been feeling well for the last few days following the game. He was suffering from chills, fatigue, fever and muscle pain. Unbeknownst to anyone, John Kizer had given his son injections of his medication. He told Bonner that he was giving him a preventative dose of malaria medicine so he would not succumb to the sickness that had taken his mother and many others. Bonner never thought of questioning his adoptive father. After all, Kizer had been a loving, even doting dad who had cared for him, taken him fishing and provided for him. Following Rosena's death, Kizer officially adopted Bonner with his grandparents' blessing. This adoption became final on October 1, 1930, when Bonner was nine. Bonner even thought of himself as lucky. After all, his father had died, followed by his mother and then his grandparents, and John Kizer was his family. John was the only parent the boy had known for the last seven years. Many people who did not care for Kizer saw his raising Bonner as proof that he was not a bad guy. After all, he was raising his dead wife's son.[103]

John Kizer, though, saw his adoption of Bonner as a means of protecting his investment. He had invested so much time and energy in marrying Rosena. Kizer profited nicely from his previous murders, but Rosena Arnold represented his most significant chance to advance his wealth. With the death of Rosena, Bonner inherited blocks 9 and 10 in the Masonic Heights subdivision in Pocahontas and hundreds of acres of prime farmland. Kizer was not about to let this child out of his clutches.[104]

Following Bonner's shoulder injury, Kizer took his son to see Dr. H.H. Price, a local chiropractor. As always, Kizer seemed opposed to traditional doctors and refused to take the boy to a physician. It is worth noting that in all the deaths associated with Kizer, he only called doctors once the patient was so sick they stood almost no chance of recovery. Price examined Bonner and quickly determined that his shoulder, while sore, was not severely injured. But during his examination, Price noticed that the young man had a badly swollen spot just below his left elbow. The doctor asked Bonner about the area, and the boy explained that his father was attempting to inoculate him against malaria. This concerned Price, who tried to talk to Kizer about his son.[105]

In the doctor's assessment, Bonner was injected with something poisoning his system. Price did not go as far as to accuse Kizer of poisoning his son, but he was concerned and urged him to take the boy to a doctor. Kizer told Dr. Price, "The boy has some ruptured blood vessels and a bad heart, which I'm afraid may become paralyzed." Soon the boy's condition worsened, and on October 19, Bonner missed school. He could not get out of bed. His condition had become much worse. By Wednesday, October 21, Bonner was dead.[106]

Bonner Kizer's death sparked the response that close-knit communities typically experience when a bright, young, popular athlete dies. People gathered around the Pocahontas Court Square to discuss and mourn Bonner. Some people naturally began to discuss the string of bad luck that John Kizer had experienced. After all, he had buried two wives and multiple family members, including the Bonners, and now his young adopted son had died in the prime of life. Before long, this talk turned to suspicion. While some people remembered that Kizer had treated each of these "beloved" family members, others began questioning that he seemed to become wealthier after each death. It did not help that Grace Adams, the woman who had escaped Kizer's clutches due to his killing of her dog, was determined to draw attention to him.[107]

10

THE LYNCH MOB

Death is a fact of life. It typically brings about sadness and mourning, but the death of a teenager often rattles a community to its core. The death of Bonner Kizer did just that in Pocahontas. Bonner was a well-liked young man in the community. He was a rising star on the football field and seemed to have a bright future. Bonner was a fixture at the soda fountain of Johnston Drug Store on Court Square and interacted with his peers and adults. The young man was mature for his age. Unfortunately, Bonner had also experienced more grief in his young life than any sixteen-year-old should have to bear. His father had died when Bonner was a young man, leaving him the heir to a substantial amount of farmland. His mother had passed away shortly after marrying his stepfather, and his Bonner grandparents had since died. Bonner's death propelled the whole community into a sense of mourning.[108]

Bonner's death also raised a large number of questions. After all, the young athlete was in excellent physical shape. Some in the community began asking questions about the deaths that seemed to follow Bonner's adoptive father, John Kizer. The more people talked, the more they concluded that there had been too many deaths for them to be coincidental. After all, Kizer had profited from many of the untimely deaths. Slowly, then more rapidly, the local community turned on John Kizer. The sixty-four-year-old "rancher" and veterinarian withdrew to his home, closing the curtains to wait out the strange looks and suspicions of townspeople and neighbors.[109]

He hid from the talk and the looks out of genuine fear. Vigilante justice was not unheard of in Pocahontas, a fact that Kizer was well aware of from the days when he had served as the chief deputy to the county sheriff. The more people suggested Bonner had been murdered and Kizer had done the deed, the more concerned the veterinarian became. People were mad as hell, and the tension was building in town. Kizer vividly remembered the night he and other deputies unsuccessfully fought off the mob that hanged George Cheverie. Hiding behind locked doors and closed drapes, Kizer feared this might be his fate.[110]

Earlier in the evening, Kizer heard that a potential mob was gathering on the court square. From his house, he could see vehicles parked with men watching his home to make sure he did not make a hasty retreat in the night. Kizer knew that his best bet was to hunker down and let the storm pass. He hoped and prayed the storm would pass.[111]

Much of what is known about the days following the death and funeral of Bonner Kizer can be found in out-of-state newspapers. While the *Pocahontas Star Herald* covered the tragic events, small-town newspapers, then as now, were reluctant to dig deep and feared alienating advertisers and subscribers. Other information comes from an unpublished manuscript found in the Randolph County Heritage Museum archives in Pocahontas, Arkansas. This sixty-page document, "John R. Kizer: A Judgement Call," written by an unknown author, examines the events following Bonner's death.[112]

Kizer was not the only individual concerned about the potential for mob violence. Randolph County sheriff John Thompson was also worried. Thompson kept an eye on the growing mob downtown and worried about what these "concerned" citizens would do if they found Kizer. Thompson intended to arrest John Kizer before the mob took matters into their own hands. This was far from the only reason for Thompson's worried state. Earlier in the day, Thompson had reviewed a report from the medical school at the University of Arkansas in Little Rock. The report's findings were clear: Bonner Kizer did not die from a football injury but from strychnine poisoning. Randolph County prosecutor George Steimel ordered the arrest of Kizer for his son's murder. But to avoid the mob and the potential for more violence, Thompson waited until late in the evening to make the arrest.[113]

Thompson first won the office of Randolph County sheriff as a Democrat in 1934. There was no other political party in the county, though a few men claimed to be Republicans. Thompson had been reelected in the Democratic primary of 1936. He appears to have been well liked and highly regarded by the public.

Sheriff Thompson and Deputy Virgil Pace drove under the cover of darkness to Kizer's home at 507 Kizer Avenue. As they approached the house, they noticed men loitering in their cars near the end of the street. The sheriff left Pace in the car to watch the potential mob and approached Kizer's door. Despite the darkness, Thompson saw clear signs that the Kizer home had been vandalized. The front of the house was spotted with eggs, tomatoes and other items thrown by passersby. Young men, many of them classmates of Bonner, as well as old men, had harassed Kizer all day. The old man's nerves were on edge as he hid in his home. As the sheriff knocked on the door, he could not help but wonder what sort of reception he would get from Kizer. Thompson and Kizer had known each other for many years. They could not be called good friends, because Kizer had few good friends. While respected in the community, he was not warm or engaging and remained aloof from most people. While few people knew Kizer well, they admired him for the way he had raised Bonner following Rosena's death. After all, Bonner was not his son. They also thought highly of him for adopting Bonner after his mother's death. By all accounts, he was a doting father. Following the young man's untimely death, many in the community began reevaluating their opinions.[114]

Kizer peered out the window in the door and saw the sheriff waiting on the porch. He reluctantly allowed Thompson inside. Kizer was known for always dressing in a neat, professional manner. He was barefoot, wearing trousers held in place by suspenders and a plain white shirt with the collar removed. Thompson noticed that Kizer's hair was a mess and that he looked as though he had spent part of the day crying. Thompson also noticed the gun the older man was holding. But the sheriff was not concerned. After all, Kizer had been harassed all day, and Thompson knew Kizer feared mob violence, for good reason. At first, Kizer failed to grasp that the sheriff was there in an official capacity. But Kizer slowly began to realize this after asking why the man was there so late.

Thompson calmly explained that according to the medical school, Bonner's death was not the result of a football injury or any other injury. Bonner had been poisoned, and Kizer was being arrested for the murder. Kizer denied any involvement in the death of Bonner. According to him, if the boy had poison in his system, he must have taken it by mistake. After all, they kept poison in the medicine cabinet. Kizer was sure Bonner had died from his injuries in the football game the previous Friday. The sheriff listened patiently to Kizer and then explained that he had to arrest the man. Ultimately, Kizer left home with the sheriff. Little did he know that he would never return to the house he valued so much with its modern conveniences. More than likely, Thompson's quick action to arrest him saved Kizer from a lynching.[115]

Small towns and communities are known for gossiping, and Pocahontas was no exception. Many residents had suspected foul play when Bonner died following a short illness. For one thing, Kizer had not sought the services of a doctor. The local post office was the center of gossip, and soon, the town was well aware that Thompson had received a report from the medical school. Morehead and others have erroneously claimed that the sheriff was notified by phone, though this is questionable, due to the lack of long-distance service even as late as 1936. Few if any states had long-distance service at this time. As word leaked that the report indicated Bonner had been murdered, anger spread. Thompson had his man in custody but was not out of the woods yet. The sheriff feared being followed. If the mob attacked the car and took Kizer, they would kill him, and there was little the lawmen could do to stop them. Locking Kizer in the local jail offered little protection. After all, mobs had previously broken prisoners out of that facility. The sheriff needed to stash the prisoner without the mob finding him.[116]

Thompson quickly devised a plan. First, he would give the mob something they wanted. He would allow them to get a quick glimpse of Kizer. This way, they would know that the man was in custody. To accomplish this, they drove from the Kizer home in South Pocahontas up the highway and past the homes of some of the small town's most affluent citizens until they reached the corner of Broadway and Bettis. From here, Thompson, Pace and Kizer could see the growing mob on the court square. This mob had been building for hours, drinking, talking and becoming agitated. Pace drove the car past the courthouse slowly so that the assembled mob could see their intended prey before Pace turned right onto Marr Street and drove the one block to the county jail. When the mob did not follow, the sheriff instructed Pace to head east toward Corning as quickly as possible. Thompson had no intention of Kizer spending a night in the Randolph County Jail. The sheriff worried that the prisoner would not survive the night if Thompson housed him locally. He also worried about being followed if he took Kizer to a neighboring county to be held. Pace drove east toward Corning. When Thompson was sure they had not been followed, he ordered Pace to turn at Reyno and go toward Maynard, in the northern part of the county.[117]

To get to Maynard, they had to cross the Current River on a ferry. At such an hour, they were the only car on the ferry, and the elderly man who operated the ferry was curious why the sheriff and his deputy were out so late. Pace was worried that the ferry operator would alert people where Kizer was. But nothing could be done. In the middle of the night, it was unlikely that the ferry operator would tell anyone, and by morning, the prisoner would be hidden temporarily in the Lawrence County Jail. The trio traveled on to Maynard, where, around 2:00 a.m., they turned back south onto the gravel road that connected Maynard to Pocahontas. As they approached Pocahontas, all three men became somewhat uneasy. Pace avoided downtown and made his way to the bridge over the Black River, then headed toward Lawrence County. Kizer was quickly deposited in the jail in Walnut Ridge. The jail was in poor shape, and this distressed the prisoner. He asked Thompson how long he would need to stay in jail. The sheriff indicated it might be weeks, much to Kizer's surprise. Once again, Kizer maintained his innocence, and the sheriff responded that if that was true, he would be out of jail soon.[118]

John Kizer had once served as a jailer in Randolph County, so jails were not new to him, though he was now locked in a filthy cell. Before heading home to Pocahontas, Thompson questioned the prisoner, asking him to tell him everything he could remember about the death of Bonner. Throughout the questioning, Kizer maintained his innocence. He said that Bonner had been taking quinine capsules for malaria. Kizer had made up the capsules for his son and prescribed them. Kizer reminded the sheriff that in the area you could not be too cautious about malaria; it killed so many. According to Kizer, the boy must have taken the wrong bottle from the bathroom medicine cabinet. It must all be a massive accident. He also said that the medical school must be mistaken; Bonner died from internal injuries he suffered in his last football game against Corning. The boy had been in pain since the football game and had been going to Dr. Price, the local chiropractor.[119]

Thompson asked about the strychnine. A local druggist at Johnston Drug Store recently reported selling Kizer the poison. Of course, Kizer claimed that he bought poison often. His use of poison to kill dogs was well known. He claimed he needed more poison for dogs and that Bonner had even helped him "put down" several dogs. At this point, Kizer even bragged about the many dogs he had killed. Thompson later noted that Kizer appeared "devoid of expression," showing no emotion. Finally, the sheriff asked bluntly, "John, did you kill Bonner?" The man looked at the sheriff coldly and said, "I did not." The sheriff began to prepare to leave but asked Kizer if he would like him to call his attorney. Kizer asked him to call Mr. Schoonover, a local attorney in Pocahontas. He also requested that Thompson notify Minnie Brown, his housekeeper, where he was. The sheriff returned to the car, where Deputy Pace was waiting patiently. As the two men drove back to Pocahontas, Pace turned to the sheriff and asked, "Well, you think he did it?" Thompson replied, "Hell, yes."[120]

Before leaving home with Sheriff Thompson the night before, Kizer had quickly written a note to Minnie. The letter indicated that he had gone away for a few days with the sheriff to avoid problems around town and asked her to take care of the house while he was gone. Minnie shared this information with others, and before long, the gossip around town was that Kizer had been arrested, though no one knew where he was being held. Mary Brown spread much of this information after talking to her friend Minnie.[121]

After Kizer had spent a few days behind bars in Walnut Ridge, Thompson moved him to the Greene County Jail in Paragould. Kizer began to doubt his ability to talk his way out of the situation. The community had turned against him and seemed unwilling to listen. The sheriff, while kind, seemed to believe the worst as well. Kizer began thinking of his future. He was reluctant to spend his life in prison, and he certainly did not want to be killed by a lynch mob and left hanging from a tree or a bridge. With these thoughts in his mind, Kizer began to consider writing a will. On the morning of November 19, 1936, he did just that. On a notepad provided by the jailer, he handwrote his last will and testament:

> *Last will and testament of John R. Kizer in his own hand-writing—Paragould Jail, November 19th 1936, time—5:00 am.*
>
> *I, John R. Kizer, being of sound mind and in good health know life is uncertain and death is shure [sic], do hereby will and bequeath to my five brothers and sisters all my property of whatever kind both real and personal in Randolph and Pulaski Counties, Arkansas. After my legal debts are paid, together with my funeral expenses then I want all my lands, about 1300 acres and all my city property as well as personal property sold and the net proceeds divided between:*
>
> *James B. Kizer, Crystal City, Mo. and Jake Kizer, Phoenix, Ariz. and Mrs Rebecca Brown, Dalton, Ark. and Mrs. Susan Toney, Dalton, Ark. and Mrs. Sarah James, McLeod, Oklahoma.*
>
> *I want my lawyers to act as my administrators without bond—*
>
> *E.G. Schoonover, E.N. Ellis, and E.V. Hoyet*
>
> *1st I want them to have a reasonable fee for the legal work they have done for me. They to determine that when all the law suites [sic] are settled up then settle with my brothers and sisters equally—after paying all the other legal indebtedness—I want my administrators to make a deed to Felix Reinick for this home in Black 10-A in Masonic Hights [sic], city of Pocahontas. He has no bond for the title but he will finish paying for his home, make him a deed.*

2nd Make deeds to all lands sold where the owners has bond for the title according to the descriptions in the title bond.
Signed this Nov. 19th. 1936
Jno R. Kizer
I therefore will and bequeath to Minnie Brown all my household goods and Ford car
Signed this Nov. 19th. 1936
Jno R. Kizer

Kizer sealed this will in an envelope and began his day.[122]

Mr. Schoonover and two associates took Kizer's case but made him pay with a chunk of his landholdings. Kizer could meet with his lawyers regularly and plan for his legal defense. Soon he would be taken back to Randolph County, where he would appear in court. According to his lawyers, Rosena's aunt Silvia Holland, who lived in St. Louis, wanted the other Bonner deaths investigated. There was talk of exhuming the bodies of Rosena, William F. Bonner and Elizebeth Bonner. Once Mrs. Holland learned that her great-nephew had been poisoned, she naturally began questioning the deaths of his mother and grandparents. Kizer learned some of this from his lawyers and some from the *Arkansas Gazette* and the *Jonesboro Sun*. Kizer seemed intrigued by the press coverage of his case, almost pleased to be so famous.

While in jail, Kizer wrote letters to friends and family, and before long, people in Pocahontas knew he was in jail in Paragould. Before long, he began to receive mail as well. One of the envelopes he received contained the following clipping from the *Pocahontas Star Herald*.

The heart of Pocahontas is bowed down. Hundreds of citizen [sic] *of Pocahontas and Randolph County paid their last tribute to "Little" Bonner Kizer, when funeral services were held in the Methodist Church last Thursday afternoon. Tear-dimmed eyes of friends and strangers alike viewed the face of all that remained of the popular 16-year-old football player who had died suddenly the week before.*

Pocahontas is accustomed to funerals but never in the history of our city has one been held that has touched more heart strings than did that of Bonner. It was different—different in more ways than one.

Sixteen years ago there was much rejoicing in the W.F. Bonner home when their petite, dark-eyed daughter, Rosena Bonner Arnold, became the mother of chubby, dimpled Bonner. The new baby was the idol of their hearts. But as the body of that same sunny boy lay in the local morgue last week, not one of those loved ones was present to drop a tear on his bier. Tom Arnold, the father, dad died when Bonner was yet a little boy. Then a few years later Rosena married John R Kizer, large landowner in the county, who was twice her age. This marriage was terminated within a few months when she, too, died after a brief and strange illness. In 1932 W.F. Bonner, the grandfather died. On July 4 of this year, Bonner came into town sobbing, "My grandmother is dead!" Her illness too had been of short duration. Then on Wednesday, Oct. 20, news spread over town that Bonner Kizer had died at the home of his stepfather after a two-day illness and without the aid of a physician. Interested citizens demanded an investigation, and the coroner's jury ordered that an autopsy be made. The results of that autopsy "that strychnine, enough to have caused death, has been found in Bonner Kizer's liver," has caused the most sensational investigation in the city's history.

Meanwhile, Bonner is sleeping in Masonic Cemetery beside those who loved him, and who were not here to place a rose on his grave.

Here's a tear for you "Little" Bonner."

Kizer read this clipping from his hometown paper and realized that he could not convince the community of his innocence.[123]

The unknown author of "John R. Kizer: A Judgement Call" claims that Mary Brown visited Kizer in the Greene County Jail. While there, she taunted Kizer with stories of how the lynch mob in Pocahontas intended to kill him. Apparently, Mary said:

I know that I shouldn't be telling you this but as a good Christian I feel I ought. When you come back to Pocahontas they's a bunch of men who are planning to string you up just like they did to George Cheverie back when we were young. You remember that don't you? That's right, you were deputy when that happened. You could not stop 'em, could you? Well, you wont be able to stop these folks either. They say if they can't get a rope around your neck before the hearing, they's going to sneak a pistol into the courthouse, or else get you afterward. I'd watch myself if I were you, John Kizer.

This news frightened Kizer. It brought back so many painful memories of the night Cheverie was lynched. Kizer knew one thing for sure: he did not plan to die at the hands of a lynch mob. Unfortunately, he also doubted the ability of local lawmen to keep him out of the hands of such a mob.[124]

Kizer was scheduled to return to Pocahontas on November 11 for a court appearance. This would be a preliminary hearing. Kizer was not the only one worried about the threat of lynching. County officials did their best to keep the time of the hearing a secret, but this proved no easy feat in Pocahontas. At the appointed time, Sheriff Thompson arrived to collect his prisoner and transport him to the courthouse in Pocahontas. Kizer saw the crowd when the car stopped on Everett Street in front of the courthouse. Naturally, he was alarmed by the size of the group but took some comfort that lynchings did not happen in broad daylight but under cover of darkness. As he exited the car, lawmen surrounded him to protect him from the jeering onlookers. This fact did not stop some in the crowd from throwing eggs and tomatoes at Kizer. The crowd included reporters from newspapers from across the nation, including the *St. Louis Post-Dispatch*, the *Chattanooga News* and the *Courier-Journal* in Louisville, Kentucky. The lawmen escorted Kizer into the building and up the stairs to the courtroom.[125]

The judge was a man named John Rogers. He had closed the courtroom to spectators, though he allowed members of the Bonner family to attend. Kizer's attorneys made a motion to delay the proceedings for a week due to a critical witness being unable to participate. George Steimel, the prosecutor, objected to the delay, and the two sides became involved in a verbal altercation. Judge Rogers eventually reestablished order, but Kizer soon rose and asked the judge for help. "Help me, Judge. They want to kill me!" Rogers asked Kizer why he thought the Bonners and community members wished to see him lynched. Kizer explained that he had been receiving hate mail since his location had been revealed. According to Kizer, many of these letters indicated a plot to kill him at this very hearing. The judge responded by ordering the spectators searched and issuing a delay until November 19.[126]

Thompson escorted the prisoner back to the car and hightailed it back to Paragould and relative safety. The judge's quickness and the fact that the crowd surrounding the courthouse had not expected Kizer to reemerge so soon may very well have saved his life. The group was unprepared, and Kizer was in the car, speeding away before they knew what was happening. Over the next week, hate mail continued to arrive. These daily letters reinforced Kizer's fear that he would be lynched soon. He even wondered that the mob might travel to Paragould and do the deed. He stopped sleeping through the night and began having nightmares about being lynched by an angry mob. The demons worsened as the day of his next hearing drew nearer. Kizer neared a nervous breakdown.

Kizer felt sure of it: As sure as he was sitting in a jail cell, the Pocahontas mob would string him up. While in jail, he wrote letters to several people. One letter was addressed to his brothers, sisters and family:

I am indeed sorry of the shame and worry that has come to you all through me. I am charged with a crime I never committed and all I ask is a fair and impartial trial and I am sure to be acquitted.

I have always lived an honest and upright life, never done a dishonest deed in my life—God bless you all. I am deeding my entire real estate of about 1,300 acres of land and some city property to my six lawyers, H.L. Ponder, H.L. Ponder, Jr., E.G. Schoonover, W.J. Schoonover, E.V. Hoyt and E.N. Ellis.

These men are to fight all my lawsuits through the courts. They are to have all the rents and profits during the litigations and when the records are cleared, they are to return to me one-half of all property deeded to them by me on October 24, 1936.

Now if anything happens to me and I go down in death, I want you, my two brothers and three sisters, to keep in touch with these three men and ask them to return to you my one-half interest which I am sure they will do.

You know my family history. Birdie Kizer and I lived together for 25 years. I treated her like a queen. She died blessing me for the good deeds done and the kindness shown her. God bless her.

Amen.

Rosena Kizer and I only had a short time together. She sang my praises daily, saying she had the nicest home in town and the best husband that ever lived.

After her death, I took her father and mother in my home and cared for them all through their lives and paid their doctor bills and funeral expenses. They died singing my praises. They loved me as their own son and I loved them as my own father and mother.

I adopted Bonner in 1930. First thing I gave him $1200 in bank stock. He was one of the nicest boys in town. He always went to Sunday School and church, always had money for his Sunday school class and always donated to any improvement to the church. He was honored and respected by his playmates and those he had personal contact with after I adopted him and began giving him money. I know I could not inherit from his estate but he could inherit from mine. In his death I have lost more than life itself—his love and companionship through life which means more than life to me.

There was never a discord between him and me. He loved, honored and respected me as his real father. He never stayed all night with a neighbor away from home but once. He and I have slept together for near on to seven years. I have washed his feet night after night when he laid down across the bed and went to sleep. Now he is gone on that long journey please bury my lifeless body in the Masonic cemetery at Pocahontas in the Armstrong plot at Rosena Kizer's feet.

God bless you all.

I have lots of good friends in Randolph County and all over the state who are praying for me that the ugly story will clear up.

Bonner went with the football team to play at Corning on Friday, October 13, and was knocked out cold by a larger boy who rammed one knee into his breast, the other into his stomach, mashing him flat as a flitter. One busted his left shoulder. In other words, they tromped him to death.

All his friends will be sorry and I am blamed for his death. Indeed I am sorry but I am not to blame in any way.

I am writing you this letter on November 12, 1936. God bless you all. All my personal property not sold at my death is to be divided equally between Minnie and Edith Brown [he later scratched out Edith] *who have been my housekeeper during my absence. God bless them both. They are requested to pay my funeral expenses not to exceed $150. D*

John R. Kizer

Based on this letter, it appears that Kizer had given up hope. In his mind, he would either be lynched or found guilty and executed for the death of Bonner Kizer.[127]

Kizer also addressed a letter to Sheriff Thompson and Randolph County coroner H.G. McNabb. This letter was written the night before his second court appearance.

Life is uncertain, death is shure—I am made to feel God Almighty has remove his shield from around me—that I am to be delivered into the hands of my enemys—if so I will resign my body to the grave and my spirit to God who gave it—Amen—If anything happens to me do not blame Mr. Thompson or anybody else for no one is to blame. Do not hold any inquest over me if you find this note on my person.

Mr. McNabb, please bury me in the Armstrong lot in the cemetery at the feet of Rosena Kizer—my dear beloved wife—I would like for Bonner to be placed between me and his grandmother Bonner—Minnie Brown will pay you out of my personal property—not to exceed $150.00

I want you and all the officers of Randolph County to know you are burying an innocent man—one who is a victim of circumstances—If Bonner died from poison he took it for quinine by mistake—the football boys killed him stomped him to death. I have been kept in jail 30 days without trial—I had rather be sleeping in my grave as to be persecuted by my fellow man without cause.

Bonner died in my arms without a struggle—with a smile on his face. He only spoke one word after I found him sitting in a rocking chair—Daddy, get me on the bed.

I cannot be cheated out of many years. I have lived a long and honorable life always doing good for evil. I hold no ill will toward you or any living person. I pray God's blessing upon you all—Amen—I truly hope you will give the papers my side of the story as they have only the bad side of the case—

I feel as I am being prosecuted for killing dogs in South Pocahontas as I have bought dozens of bottles of Strychnine in past years. Our farm comes up to the south end of the city and the last strychnine that was put out for dogs was bought from Bill Bates at the Johnston Drug Store. Three weeks later I bought another bottle from Rector Johnson for the rats in the junkhouse and the sparrow birds—Bonner handled both bottles—killed seven dogs and there was some left in the last bottle and he set it in the medicine case where there was more than fifty bottles of quinine. Dr. Price gave him adjustments; he would not have Dr. Baltz for anyone else. Said the athletic association paid for his adjustments. In losing Bonner I have lost a companion for life—I have also lost all the property I have given him which is small compared to his live—I loved the little fellow Dearly—he is sleeping with the angels in heaven now I desire to follow him in death—God Bless him—and I am asking God in his mercy to forgive the sins of my enemys who have said ugly words about me—amen—our Lord and Savior Jesus said—greater love has no man than this—that he will lay down his life for the loved ones—Amen—

In laying down my life in this world I will pick up again Beyond the Skies eternal in the Heavens—

This is being written late at night November 18, 1936—Knowing I am to face the court tomorrow—I am going in with clean hands and an honest heart. I do not fear the outcome of the case as I know God and Justice is on my side and I am bound to win. God Bless the Court and all the court officials of Randolph County—Amen.

Jno. R. Kizer
My admrs will pay my funeral expenses.
Jno. R. Kizer

Kizer had a plan. All of his life, he liked to be in control. He was a master manipulator, and being locked in a cell where almost all control had been taken from him was too much to handle. On the morning of November 19, Kizer ate breakfast in his cell after sleeping little the night before. A guard brought him a change of clothing that his lawyers wanted Kizer to wear for his court appearance. Dressed in clean clothing, Kizer carefully placed the will and letters in his coat pocket, where they would indeed be found. Just as he was about to leave the cell, Kizer retrieved a small package he had kept hidden, in preparation for this day. The car taking Kizer to his hearing moved slowly out of Paragould. The road to Walnut Ridge could have been better. At Walnut Ridge, the route to Pocahontas was better. As they approached Walnut Ridge, Kizer's mood changed. He seemed lost in thought and then asked the sheriff if it would be possible to get a haircut and shave before appearing in court. Thompson took the prisoner to a barbershop on Second Street in Walnut Ridge. While getting his hair cut, Kizer purchased a soda. Before he left the shop, he used the bathroom. He carried what was left of his soda to the bathroom, but no one thought about it.[128]

In the bathroom of the barbershop, Kizer examined himself in the mirror. He thought back to the nightmares he had been dealing with. Kizer relived every moment of that fateful night when he and the other deputies could not stop an angry mob from breaking George Cheverie out of jail and hanging him. He vividly remembered helping cut down Cheverie's bloated stiff body from the bridge over Marr Creek. He saw that night as a failure; he and others could not stop the lynching. For several nights he had been awakened by a vivid dream in which he was helping lift the body of a lynched man. When he saw the face, it was him. He simply would not allow a lynch mob to do that to him. He would take control of his life one last time. He pulled a small bottle from his pocket as if unsure of his actions. Thompson and the other lawmen had not noticed this bottle. Kizer removed a few dusty capsules from the bottle and examined them in his hand. Before he could change his mind, he swallowed the first capsule and quickly followed it with two more. He thought for a moment of making himself throw up, but then he remembered it was this or the mob, at least in his eyes. This way, he was in control.[129]

Kizer rode to Pocahontas in silence. The sheriff thought Kizer seemed at peace with whatever had happened in court. Kizer was at peace. He knew that he had taken matters into his own hands and that no mob would pass judgment on him. Kizer began to feel pain as they drove over the Black River Bridge at Pocahontas. Each of the three capsules he took in Walnut Ridge contained enough strychnine to kill a man. As they pulled up in front of the Randolph County Courthouse, he began to have severe convulsions, like those Birdie had experienced and, later, Rosena and Bonner. As news cameras flashed, John Kizer's suffering was captured for the world to see. The policemen carried him across the square, down Bettis Street to the office of Dr. Mathis Baltz. Time seemed to stop as the crowd watched. The man they had come to see was carried into the doctor's office. Soon an ambulance from McNabb Funeral Home arrived and took Kizer's body away. The letters and will were found just as he had intended. The sheriff, Prosecuting Attorney George Steimel and others took the notes and will to Steimel's office, which overlooked the square.[130]

Due to the nature of the death, an autopsy was necessary. It concluded that John Kizer had committed suicide by strychnine, the very poison he was accused of using on his victims. His death made headlines across the South: "Murder Defendant Believed to Have Committed Suicide Day of Hearing," "Planter Takes Life Before Murder Trial," "Death Ends Trial of Poison Slayer" and "Dies on Arrival at Court for Trial." McNabb Funeral Home embalmed John Kizer; after all, he had paid for so many funerals and waited for some family member to claim the body. For a while, it looked like no one would claim the body. Then Kizer's brother John showed up. Kizer had requested to be buried with Rosena and Bonner, but that was out of the question. In a small service attended by just a handful of family members, he was buried in the Reynolds Cemetery near Dalton, where he grew up.[131]

11

STRYCHNINE

John Kizer would hurt no one else, but questions remained. How many people did he kill? How did he get strychnine while in the Greene County Jail? Our unnamed author provides a possible explanation: Mary Brown. Mary Brown immensely disliked John Kizer and thought he was capable of murder. The day after his arrest, Mary visited the Kizer home. She was on friendly terms with Minnie Brown, his housekeeper. During Mary's visit, Minnie left the home briefly, leaving a very suspicious Mary unattended. She searched the house and found a small bottle of strychnine in the bathroom medicine cabinet. For Mary, this was all the proof she needed. Rather than tell the sheriff about the poison, she slipped it in her pocket and took it.[132]

Mary's Arkoma Café was a hot spot in Pocahontas for gossip, and Mary seemed to pick up on the latest stories around town. She heard all the chatter about Kizer and the death of Bonner. Since she never liked the man, she had no trouble believing he could have or did murder his wives, in-laws and son. No one knew where Kizer was being held for the first few days following his arrest. Soon, word spread that he was in the Greene County Jail. Mary Brown made two trips to see the man she despised. She gave Kizer the bottle from his bathroom when she went, whispering, "Do the right thing." She also talked to him at length about how mad the community was and about the volumes of hate mail. This affected Kizer. He took the bottle—the very one he more than likely used to poison Bonner—and quickly hid it in his cell. This bottle was lost to history until January 17, 2019. One of the state troopers who escorted Kizer on that fateful day was Elbert Frazier. Frazier was either the fourth or fifth Arkansas Ranger/trooper ever hired. The Arkansas Rangers eventually became the Arkansas State Police; its members are often called state troopers. Frazier was with Kizer when he died and took part in searching for his effects following his death. Years later, Frazier's son found the small bottle his father had kept all those years. As he began to research, he concluded that the bottle was connected to the John Kizer case that his dad had spoken of on many occasions. The bottle was donated to the Randolph County Heritage Museum, where it became part of the John Kizer story.[133]

When Bonner Kizer died, his father became his heir. At his father's death, Bonner had inherited significant real estate in the form of farmland and city lots. When John Kizer was arrested and charged with Bonner's death, the court appointed A.J. Cole to administer the estate of Bonner Kizer. Cole wasted little time, and on October 28, 1936, he filed a suit in circuit court in Randolph County against John Kizer for damages for the pain and suffering endured by Bonner Kizer. The court found in favor of the Bonner Kizer estate for $17,500. By this time, John Kizer had committed suicide, and his estate, represented by Ben A. Brown, appealed the ruling, arguing that the court should not have ruled against Kizer, as he was dead. First, Brown argued that no action could be taken, since the person causing the pain and suffering was no longer living. Second, he argued that Cole could not sue Bonner, since Bonner was legally Kizer's son. The Arkansas Supreme Court found that the court had not erred and refused to overturn the initial ruling.[134]

The Randolph County Heritage Museum contains an exhibit about crime and law enforcement in the county. John R. Kizer is a source of significant interest to museum visitors. With the rise of heritage tourism, Pocahontas embraced ghost tours, and the story of Kizer figures prominently in these activities. People retain a morbid fascination with Kizer and his victims, leading to feature stories in magazines and newspapers over the years. Despite its many flaws, the most prominent account has always been "They Died Like Dogs" in *True Detective*. Today, the land in South Pocahontas that was once part of the Kizer farm is a subdivision.

Greed consumed John Kizer and led to what remains the worst series of killings to ever occur in Randolph County. It is hard to imagine how the love of money would drive a man to murder his wife of twenty-five years, along with other people who loved him. The murder of sixteen-year-old Bonner finally turned the community against Kizer and brought the world he had built out of so much suffering to an end. Viewed through a modern lens, it is hard to fathom how so many deaths occurred without raising more suspicion than they did. To understand this, we must view these crimes from the perspective of the era in which they took place. Rural Arkansas, like much of rural America, was slow to embrace some of the advancements of the Progressive Era, modern technology was not available and laws in effect today requiring autopsies and investigations had not been enacted.

While greed explains the crimes, psychological or mental issues must also be considered. Many people are greedy without murdering loved ones to cash in insurance policies. Early in Kizer's life, we see the disturbing tendency to kill dogs simply because he hated the animals. This demonstrates a callous disregard for life in general. While his statements about dogs being bad for running cattle are true, and while he is far from the only person who killed animals that interfered with livestock, he seems to have taken pleasure in killing. This gives us an insight into his psychological makeup and raises questions worth further exploration.

At the time of Kizer's death, greed seemed the most plausible explanation for his gruesome actions. Rumors swirled concerning his money, and more than one individual sought to find the supposed hiding place for his ill-gotten gains. Some claimed that he had cash in the bank, but this rumor proved unfounded. Other people argued that Kizer had buried large amounts of gold at his home. One story claimed that more than $3,400 worth of gold was buried at his home south of town, quite a sum during the Depression. This gold would be worth more than $74,000 in 2023. Such a rumor interested many in the community. According to the United Press, when men arrived at the Kizer home, they found a "Gaping Hole" where the gold was believed to be hidden. This story is unsubstantiated but provides an interesting final twist to the tale.[135]

The Great Depression and the significant financial losses sustained by Kizer help explain some of his murders, but not all of them. The first murders occurred before the stock market crash, during much more prosperous economic times. Kizer likely suffered minor financial setbacks that drove him to commit these crimes and collect on these insurance policies. By the time the stock market crashed in 1929, he had become more desperate. He, like many Americans, found himself wiped out. In Kizer's case, his land was so encumbered by debt that he had no financial flexibility. As Randolph County banks closed, he also lost what money he had in those institutions.

Following the crash, Kizer was more than $80,000 in debt, and he recouped much of that through his crimes.

Over the years, the story of John R. Kizer and his notorious crimes has taken on a life of its own. Authors such as Morehead and others have exaggerated the story. Morehead added victims to make the tale more compelling, changed names and visualized much of the story. It made for good copy and fed into Americans' obsession with true crime narratives. Following the publication of his "They Died Like Dogs," Morehead's account slowly became the dominant version of events, eclipsing the true story. The actual history was bad enough. In a rush to embrace heritage tourism, Pocahontas has propagated this false narrative through ghost tours and booklets for sale at the local museum and has helped retell the story in multiple publications. The true story emerges only after careful examination of census records, marriage records, death certificates, divorce filings, court cases and newspaper accounts. What appears is a riveting tale of greed, murder and deception.

NOTES

Introduction

1. Tom Dillard, "Neighborhoods Filled with Houseboats," *Northwest Arkansas Democrat Gazette*, March 3, 2019.
2. "A Ghost on the Black River," *Arkansas Democrat Gazette*, April 29, 2020.
3. "George Shivery (Lynching of)," *Encyclopedia of Arkansas*, www.encyclopediaofarkansas.net, May 7, 2023.
4. Ibid.
5. "Slayton Released on $25,000 Bond," *Hope Star*, February 11, 1932; Slayton vs. State of Arkansas, 53 S.W. 2d 13 (Ark. 1932).
6. "The Murder of Manley Jackson: Articles and Clippings on the Murder of Marshal Jackson, Slain by the Notorious Freddy Barker in 1931" (Pocahontas, AR: Publication of Five Rivers Historic Preservation Inc.)
7. "Cora Hebner: Gorgeous & Deadly," publication of Five Rivers Historic Preservation Inc.
8. Ibid.
9. Ibid.
10. Ibid.
11. Marr, "Long Life and Quiet Death of *True Detective* Magazine."
12. Ibid.
13. Morehead, "They Died Like Dogs"; "John R. Kizer: A Judgement Call"; "For the Love of Money," *AY About You*, October 1, 2019.

Chapter 1

14. Dalton, *History of Randolph County*, 5.

15. Ibid., 9–11.

16. H.L. Zimmer, "Mistress of Tragedy."

17. Ibid., 138.

18. Ibid., 173–79, 183.

19. Ibid., 183.

20. "REACH," Black River Technical College, www.blackrivertech.org, accessed May 8, 2023.

21. Dalton, *History of Randolph County*, 47–54.

22. Ibid., 55.

23. Ibid., 16–20.

24. Ibid., 24–25.

25. Ibid., 235–38, 172–73.

26. Dalton, *History of Randolph County*, 66–71.

27. Ibid.

28. Ibid., 81–87.

29. Dalton, *History of Randolph County*, 194–97.

30. Ibid., 58–60.

31. Ibid., 54–57, 46.

32. Ibid., 235–38.

33. Ibid., 231–35.

34. Ibid., 219.

35. Ibid., 224–30.

Chapter 2

36. Dalton, *History of Randolph County*, 215–30.

37. U.S. Census, 1880, 1890, 1900.

38. Ibid., 81–87.

39. Photo in the collection of the Randolph County Heritage Museum.

40. 1860 U.S. Census, 1880 U.S. Census, 1900 U.S. Census, 1910 U.S. Census.

41. U.S. Confederate Soldiers Compiled Service Records, 1861–1865, Ancestry.com, accessed February 8, 2023.

42. U.S. Compiled Marriages from Select Counties, 1779–1992, Ancestry.com., accessed February 8, 2023; U.S. Census 1850.

43. U.S. Index of death records.
44. U.S. Census, 1900.
45. Morehead, "They Died Like Dogs"; U.S. Index of Marriages; U.S. Index of Divorces.
46. Morehead, "They Died Like Dogs."

Chapter 3

47. Kenneth Bridges, "Malaria," *Encyclopedia of Arkansas*, accessed May 9, 2023; Ken Bridges, "Malaria a Deadly Scourge in Arkansas for Many Years," *El Dorado News-Times*, July 21, 2020; Tom Dillard, "Mosquitoes Were Curse to Early Arkansas," *Arkansas Democrat Gazette*, August 18, 2019.
48. J.N. Hays, *Epidemics and Pandemics: Their Impacts on Human History* (Santa Barbara, CA: ABC-CLIO, 2005), 10–12.
49. "Smallpox," *Encyclopedia of Arkansas*, accessed May 9, 2023; Bridges, "Malaria."
50. Rodney Harris, "Maynard Baptist Academy," *Encyclopedia of Arkansas*, accessed May 9, 2023.
51. Bridges, "Malaria a Deadly Scourge."
52. Ibid.

Chapter 4

53. "Alleged Prisoner Profited $60,000 from Six Deaths," *St. Louis Post-Dispatch*, November 20, 1936; Morehead, "They Died Like Dogs."
54. Morehead, "They Died Like Dogs."
55. Ibid.
56. Ibid.
57. U.S. Census records, 1900, 1910, 1920, 1930.
58. "Alleged Poisoner Profited."
59. Undated obituary of Robert Edwin Anderson in the *Pocahontas Star Herald*, 1926, month unknown.
60. Morehead, "They Died Like Dogs."
61. Morehead, "They Died Like Dogs"; U.S. Divorce index, 1923–1939; U.S. Census 1900; U.S. Find a Grave Index, 1600s–current; U.S. Census 1920; U.S. Select Death Index, 1907–1960.
62. Morehead, "They Died Like Dogs."

63. U.S. Census 1920; Arkansas Death Certificates, 1914–69.

Chapter 5

64. Gail S. Murray, "Forty Years Ago: The Great Depression Comes to Arkansas," *Arkansas Historic Quarterly*, Winter 1970, 291.
65. Murray, "Forty Years Ago."
66. Southern Arkansas University, www.saumag.edu, accessed June 10, 2023.
67. Ibid.; "$60,000 from Six Deaths," *St. Louis Post-Dispatch*, November 30, 1936.
68. "Alleged Poisoner."
69. Ronald Hosey, *History of the Bank of Pocahontas*, Randolph County Heritage Museum; "Banking in Randolph County," Randolph County Heritage Museum.

Chapter 6

70. Newspaper ads from the files of the Randolph County Heritage Museum Archives.
71. Morehead, "They Died Like Dogs."
72. Land deeds from multiple transactions found in the files of the Randolph County Heritage Museum Archives.
73. U.S. Census Records, 1920.
74. Obituary of Mrs. Birdie Kizer, *Pocahontas Star Herald*, December 29, 1927.
75. Morehead, "They Died Like Dogs."
76. Ibid.
77. Morehead, "They Died Like Dogs."
78. "Our Story," Stbernards.info, accessed May 15, 2023.
79. Morehead, "They Died Like Dogs."
80. "Mrs. Kizer Buried," *Pocahontas Star Herald*, December 29, 1927.
81. U.S. Census 1920.
82. Morehead, "They Died Like Dogs."
83. Nancy Hendricks, "Flood of 1927," *Encyclopedia of Arkansas*, accessed May 29, 2023.

Chapter 7

84. U.S. Census, 1900, 1910, 1920.
85. Wedding announcement found in the records of the Randolph County Heritage Museum.
86. U.S. Index of Divorces.
87. "Deaths of Two Women Probed for Poisoning," *Chattanooga News*, November 18, 1936.
88. Ibid.
89. "Alleged Poisoner Profited."
90. Ibid.
91. Obituary of Rosena Kizer, Randolph County Heritage Museum Archives.
92. "Alleged Poisoner Profited."

Chapter 8

93. Brown v. Cole.
94. Ibid.
95. Ibid.
96. Ibid.
97. "Alleged Poisoner Profited."
98. "Death Ends Trial of Poison Slayer: Collapses on Way to Face Count of Poisoning 16-Year Old Step-Son," *Kingsport Times*, November 19, 1936.

Chapter 9

99. Brown v. Cole, 198 Ark.417.
100. Ibid.
101. "John R. Kizer: A Judgement Call"; "Alleged Poisoner Profited."
102. "Alleged Poisoner Profited."
103. "John R. Kizer: A Judgement Call."
104. Brown v. Cole, 198 Ark.417.
105. Ibid.
106. Ibid.
107. "Alleged Poisoner Profited."

Chapter 10

108. "John R. Kizer: A Judgement Call."
109. Ibid.; "Alleged Poisoner Profited."
110. "John R. Kizer: A Judgement Call."
111. Ibid.
112. Ibid.
113. Ibid.; "Alleged Poisoner Profited."
114. "John R. Kizer: A Judgement Call."
115. Ibid.
116. Ibid.
117. Ibid.
118. Ibid.
119. Ibid.
120. Ibid.
121. Ibid.
122. Last Will and Testament of John R. Kizer, Randolph County Heritage Museum Archives.
123. "Bonner Kizer," *Pocahontas Star Herald*, October 1936.
124. "John R. Kizer: A Judgement Call."
125. "Alleged Poisoner Profited"; "John R. Kizer: A Judgement Call."
126. Ibid.
127. Letter from John R. Kizer, Randolph County Heritage Museum.
128. Ibid.
129. "John R. Kizer: A Judgement Call."
130. Ibid.
131. Ibid.

Chapter 11

132. "John R. Kizer: A Judgement Call."
133. Frazier, interview by Steve Shults.
134. Brown v. Cole; "Gaping Hole Greets Searchers for Gold," United Press, newspaper unknown, Randolph County Heritage Museum Archives.
135. "Gaping Hole Greets Searchers for Gold," *Knoxville News Sentinel*, December 13, 1936.

BIBLIOGRAPHY

Newspapers

Arkansas Democrat Gazette (Little Rock, AR)
Chattanooga (TN) News
El Dorado (AR) News-Times
Hope (AR) Star
Kingston (TN) Times
Knoxville (TN) News Sentinel
Northwest Arkansas Democrat Gazette (Fayetteville, AR)
Pocahontas (AR) Star Herald
St. Louis Post-Dispatch

Government Documents

Brown v. Cole, Arkansas Supreme Court, May 29, 1939.
Encyclopedia of Arkansas. www.encyclopediaofarkansas.net.
Randolph County Heritage Museum Archives. www.randolphcomuseum.org.
U.S. Census Records. www.archives.gov/research/census.
U.S. Index of Death Records. www.archives.gov/research/vital-records.
U.S. Index of Divorces. www.archives.gov/research/vital-records.
U.S. Index of Marriages. www.archives.gov/research/vital-records.

Books, Articles and Interviews

Black River Technical College. "Rice-Upshaw House." www.blackrivertech.org.

Dalton, Lawrence. *A History of Randolph County*. Little Rock, AR: Democrat Printing Company, 1945.

Frazier, Elbert. Interview by Steve Shults. January 17, 2019.

"John R. Kizer: A Judgement Call." Unpublished manuscript. Randolph County Heritage Museum.

Marr, John. "The Long Life and Quiet Death of *True Detective* Magazine." *Gizmodo*, August 19, 2015.

Morehead, Charles. "They Died Like Dogs." *True Detective*, April 1957.

St. Bernard's Hospital. "Our Story." www.stbernards.info.

ABOUT THE AUTHOR

Dr. Rodney Harris earned a PhD in history from the University of Arkansas at Fayetteville, an MA in history from the University of Central Arkansas and a BA in political science from Arkansas State University in Jonesboro. Harris is currently the History and Political Science Department chair at Williams Baptist University in Walnut Ridge, Arkansas. He specializes in southern political and religious history, particularly how the two intersect.

Harris is also the president and CEO of Five Rivers Historic Preservation Inc. and the Randolph County Heritage Museum in his hometown, Pocahontas, Arkansas. He is a trustee of the Arkansas Historical Association and the Wings of Honor World War II Museum in Walnut Ridge. Harris is a past vice-chair of the Arkansas State Review Board for Historic Preservation and has served as an advisor for multiple museums and organizations. He is the author of *Images of America: Pocahontas and Randolph County* and numerous articles and chapters.

Harris and his wife, Kristi, have known each other since the second grade and have two children, Trae and Will. They live in Pocahontas, Arkansas.